Praise for *Letters from Wankie*—

"A gorgeous, touching, tragic tale of a lost — but now, thanks to Patricia Friedberg — never forgotten time in a remote corner of colonial Africa."

—Douglas Rogers, *New York Times* journalist and author of *The Last Resort: A Memoir of Zimbabwe*

"Patricia Friedberg's *Letters from Wankie*, her memoir of starting married life in colonial Rhodesia with her newly minted doctor husband, is a delightful account of a plucky young woman who takes things as they come and makes the best of them. She effectively uses the device of letters to home to set up her story. Then, for her readers, she fills in the backstory she didn't want her parents to know.

"Patricia's 'voice' made me smile all through her account of life in Wankie, which one of the book's characters calls 'the hell hole of Rhodesia.' As she ponders spending two years there she asks herself: Why on earth hadn't I asked a few questions beforehand? Like do we have a house with a proper roof? Or . . . Was there a psychiatrist or a marriage counselor I could speak with, if need be?

"Her descriptions of her job at the Native Affairs Department are priceless (and certainly accurate). Each day she is called on to work with the local tribesmen who arrive inside her office with whole families, including their livestock: 'I raced to retrieve the recently signed copy of the European marriage certificate from the mouth of an oversized Billy goat. The cow wouldn't stop mooing, her udders just about reaching the ground. Will someone please milk that cow?'

"Reading *Letters from Wankie* is like listening to a charming tale told by a good friend — and, throughout the book, Friedberg exhibits the knack of making you feel she's a friend you have known forever.

"Well done!"

—Georgia Court, owner, Bookstore 1 Sarasota

"What an adventure! I loved this book! I could not stop reading this honestly portrayed, exhilarating account of Patricia Friedberg's journey into the interior of Africa in the fifties. Filled with humour and astute wry observations, this is a delightful trip into the past where a newly married and naive British woman is taken by her new husband to live in a town in the middle of Africa, where elephants stop trains from running, where insects and lizards outnumber their human cohabitants, where baboon tails are collected for money. No sooner than she arrives in this desolate and isolated mining town with the dubious name of Wankie, she is given

having to administer and preside over cases of theft, infidelity, marriage and injustice.

"The letters, documents and photos interspersed throughout the book reveal it to be a valuable slice of history that documents an era now washed away, an insight into a country which was once the jewel of Africa, and now is in ruins."

—Paul Williams, Ph.D., author of *Soldier Blue*

"*Letters from Wankie*, by Patricia Friedberg, is a spell-binding memoir about herself as a twenty-year-old bride in 1954, who leaves her loving Jewish family in London to move with her new, handsome, Jewish doctor husband to his post in the tiny mining town of Wankie in Rhodesia, Africa. In her 'home' — two connecting thatched huts with earth floors — she battles mosquitoes, snakes, lizards and the occasional bullfrog. She also confronts a changing cast of fascinating humans, both Europeans (whites) and Natives (blacks), who need her help as Clerk of the Court of the Native Commissioners Office, a job she landed because she could type.

"Based on letters the author sent to her parents during her two-year 'tour,' the book is augmented with candid observations about why the future of Africa would eventually change: short-sightedness of colonialism; Europeans' inhuman treatment of Natives, who were their servants, a practice she hated; and the futile nature of most missionary efforts.

"Read it and cheer for a young, brave and honest twenty-year old who used her brain, heart and the 'old British try,' to make a diffe.rence in Africa. Without computers!"

—Joan Kufrin, author of *Uncommon Women*
and *Leo Burnett, Star-Reacher*

"*Letters from Wankie* originated when a twenty-year-old bride took pen in hand. It was a stroke of good fortune that her mum retained the letters she wrote. The information provided is not the same old, same old. Now apply the finely honed writing skills of a mature Patricia Friedberg to the business of writing this memoir, and you can't miss. Ms. Friedberg peppers her recollections with mental scenery that is thought-provoking, instructs and entertains. Exceedingly well done and a pleasure to read."

—Marilyn Pincus, bestselling author, ghostwriter and
member of the Authors Guild, New York, NY

LETTERS
FROM
WANKIE

A Place in Colonial Africa

Patricia Friedberg

Rainbow Books, Inc.
FLORIDA

Softcover ISBN 978-1-56825-165-3
EPUB eBook ISBN 978-1-56825-166-0

Letters from Wankie:
A Place in Colonial Africa
Copyright © 2013 by Patricia Friedberg

Author's Website: PatriciaFriedberg.com

Front cover designed by Michael Peters.

Published by

Rainbow Books, Inc.
P. O. Box 430
Highland City, FL 33846-0430
RainbowBooksInc.com

Editorial Offices and Wholesale/Distributor Orders

Telephone (863) 648-4420, Fax (863) 647-5951, RBIbooks@aol.com

Individuals' Orders

https://www.createspace.com/4329142
amazon.com, AllBookStores.com

Other than Neville Sherlock and family members, the names of the people portrayed in *Letters from Wankie* have been changed. The stories related are true and taken from the two years the author worked as Clerk of the Court at the Native Commissioners Office in Wankie, Rhodesia. All images not otherwise credited are the property of the author.

Trade Softcover Edition 2013
Produced and Printed in the United States of America.

For my grandchildren:
Jessica, Max, Isabella, Sofia, Raffaella, Oliver,
Joshua, Jenna and great grandson Mason

And you calling me colored??

When I born, I black.

When I grow up, I black.

When I go in sun, I black.

When I scared, I black.

When I sick, I black.

And when I die, I still black.

And you white people.

When you born, you pink.

When you grow up, you white.

When you go in sun, you red.

When you cold, you blue.

When you scared, you yellow.

When you sick, you green

And when you die, you grey . . .

And you calling me colored??

—Anonymous

By the same author

Novel

21 Aldgate (Rainbow Books, Inc., 2010)

Illustrated Children's Books

*Dear Jake: A Letter to a Grandchild
of Divorcing Parents* (BookSurge.com, 2008)

*Dear Sammy: A Letter to a Grandchild
of Divorcing Parents* (BookSurge.com, 2008)

Screenplays

Journey from the Jacarandas (1997)

Progress of the Sun (2004)

21 Aldgate (2008)

Columns

"Lands End to Lands End" columnist

for the *Longboat Observer* (1982–1986)

CONTENTS

Preface

Eight years after my father died my mother passed away. They had lived all their lives in London and had moved only twice in their long marriage. It had come time for me to sell what could be sold, pack what I chose to keep and give to charity shops anything they might deem profitable for their organizations. In a bottom drawer of my parents' dressing table I found love letters they had sent to each to each other when they were courting and, to my surprise, bundles of blue air letters I'd mailed from Rhodesia, where I began my married life. The love letters I set aside, feeling it too soon to intrude on their privacy. The air letters intrigued me. I stopped what I was doing, untied the string around the first bundle and began to read.

One after another gave a glimpse into colonial Africa in the mid-fifties. There were spelling mistakes and grammatical errors, but none of that mattered. Memories flooded back — had I really been that person in that small "town" called Wankie? I had in my hands a personal account of those colonial years. I packed the letters carefully and took them back to the States, where I filed them away, thinking perhaps they, like my parents' letters, would make interesting reading for my children and grandchildren in years to come.

I've returned to Rhodesia (Zimbabwe) a number of times and seen the devastation brought about by Robert Mugabe and his henchmen. I thought once again about my letters, particularly the last one in the bundles my mother had kept so safely.

✉

Dear Mummy and Daddy,

You can now close the file of correspondence and put it away somewhere very safe so that in years to come we can look back on pleasant and exciting memories . . .

Letters from Wankie has been both a duty and a lesson that I felt more and more compelled to write. It tells the truth about one small area of Africa at a time when a country named Rhodesia had a promising future. Today, Zimbabwe teeters on the edge of starvation and ruin. It is not the country I left all those years ago.

I recognize the word *Native* used throughout *Letters from Wankie* is now considered politically incorrect, and I apologize to any who find the word offensive. In colonial Africa, the term Native was commonly used to distinguish one race from the other. Native referred to the indigenous African, while *European* described anyone white, though not necessarily of European background.

LETTERS
FROM
WANKIE

INTRODUCTION

My father, a discontented furrier, dreamt of moving to Australia after the end of World War II. For ten pounds the Australian government offered to pay the remainder of the fare on any ocean liner heading for the spectacular beaches of Bondi. You could immigrate with your family to a far off place little touched by war. A land of sunshine, a land of immigrants, a land still considered British. My father envisaged himself farming somewhere in the outback, raising mink or better lambs, growing vegetables, wearing an Aussie hat. My parents discussed the idea every evening after he came home from work. But . . .

What if they made the wrong move? How could they leave their families? Australia might as well have been the moon, it was so far away; yet, it was an opportunity not to be missed. It became an agonizing, ever present dilemma — of could they, should they?

Would their daughters be happy? Would they be happy?

Mother left the final decision to her husband. She would no longer try to persuade him.

Dad coped with the responsibility in a strange way. No more discussion meant he had to come up with an answer. He meditated by the rose bushes in the garden. He took long walks in the fields behind our house. He did the "on the one hand —" thing and the "on the other hand —" thing. A man who loved the outside and all things natural had worked every day in his family's fur factory. He was a master cutter, learned it at his grandfather's knee, so to speak, and he loathed every minute of the time he spent in that dark and dingy setting. He finally chose to stay in the land of his birth because he was afraid to move from the known to the unknown.

I had my own dream to travel: to go to America, to visit New York, see Hollywood, stand on the Golden Gate Bridge and gaze over the Pacific Ocean. I accomplished that twenty-five years later, though without the enthusiasm I once had. Not for one moment did I ever give a thought to living in Africa. In my mind you had to be an explorer or a film maker to venture there. Like many others I thought of Africa as one huge, forbidding Dark Continent — never separating it into countries or cities.

Stanley and Livingstone met there. Film maker John Huston deposited Humphrey Bogart and Katherine Hepburn in a dilapidated boat, *The African Queen*, to chug down the Zambezi among threatening creatures large and small. And who could forget Tarzan, swinging from trees to save any white damsel in distress. (Yes, she had to be white.)

Even my dad's uncle landed up in Africa, though not by his own volition — he was sent as a soldier to help relieve Mafeking during the Boer War. I don't think he got anywhere near Mafeking; in fact, the day he arrived on the African continent, the siege ended. Boldly he stood with pith helmet in hand under a palm tree in a treasured family photo. I don't recall seeing any palm trees in Mafeking a half a century later. They probably dropped his platoon off in Egypt.

Yet there I was, barely twenty years old, a Londoner starting married life on board a ship bound for Africa, and that's when I began my letters home.

I met my future husband at a wedding held at the Savoy Hotel in London. My aunt, the family matchmaker, had arranged for me to meet a young doctor named Dennis, who was supposed to look for me after the meal. Whether he did I'll never know because a good looking South African named David greeted me as I walked into the main ballroom and wouldn't leave my side. He said later he knew immediately he'd met the girl he intended to marry. He also knew it might mean enduring another British winter to convince her.

Despite the weather, the rationing and the lack of sunshine, David loved London. He'd left his native South Africa to further his medical career and to get the coveted MRCP, Membership in the Royal College of Physicians. That he'd achieved, and now he had to make a choice: stay and put up with the miserable British climate or return to Johannesburg. He chose to hang on in London to woo the young woman he was determined to marry.

David phoned every day, took me to the pictures to see *Hans Christian Andersen* (my choice, not his). He introduced me to live performances of Beethoven and Brahms. He knew every play Shakespeare had ever written and quoted poetry at the drop of a hat. He was unlike any other boy I'd dated — he'd come from South Africa and customs, perhaps, were different there.

He told me his mother Violet was a teacher. She taught David at home and loved the classics. She died just before his twentieth birthday, five years previous, and he still missed her terribly. His dad Sam served in North Africa in the air force — hadn't been back long. David was not as close to Sam as he had been to his mother. Recently, Sam had married Pauline, who'd been after him for quite a while, which made his son feel less guilty about leaving him. They settled in the same flat he and his mother shared while Sam was away fighting the war in North Africa. Actually Sam never held a gun or fought anyone; his assignment to the Quarter Master's Store had him allocating government issue to the battalions fighting Rommel's troops in the desert.

My mother's family were secular Jews. They celebrated the High Holidays, Rosh Hashanah and Yom Kippur, and loved Passover. Their way of thinking was to let the orthodox observe Tisha B'Av, Purim and Sukkot. They were satisfied with what they considered sufficient observance. My grandma, a Londoner through and through, didn't understand a word of

Yiddish and remained a Cockney at heart. She wouldn't think
of going without a Christmas tree and a goose for dinner on
that very English traditional holiday. My father, the pious one,
attended synagogue every Saturday morning and prayed on
behalf of the lot of us.

I attended Hebrew school for years, all through the war.
Three times a week I went unwillingly to shul. Not only was it
dangerous to be out in the early evening because of the bomb-
ing, it was also boring when I got to class. I couldn't understand
a word the German refugee Rabbi said — either in English or
Hebrew. He would stand at the blackboard and rant and rave,
I think in Yiddish — it could have been Chinese as far as I was
concerned. I did eventually manage to learn the Hebrew alpha-
bet, though by the end of my "incarceration" it still took me
forever to sound out each word. At the age of twelve I sounded
like a four-year-old, phonetically pronouncing every syllable.
And at the age of thirty-something, when I first visited Israel, I
still sounded out each Hebrew letter. I proudly read the word
Eget on every bus in Israel and thought that was its destination, until I was informed it happened to be the name of the
bus company. I took taxis after that.

Shortly after we met, David accepted a six week locum in
Nottingham, but it didn't stop him from staying in contact. My
parents were more impressed than I was — his letters were long
and full of quotations from romantic poets. When he returned
to London we met for lunch just about every day, and it was
obvious his was not just a passing phase.

Foremost in the suitor category for young women of
marriageable age were doctors. David had all the necessary
qualifications to answer the prayers of all Jewish mothers. My
aunt, the matchmaker, had failed with Dennis. He was out of
the running, and David had taken his place. There were many
eyewitness accounts of that fateful evening when I entered The
Savoy Hotel, much of it retold in various dramatic renditions to
my parents. "Love at first sight," and it continued from there.

"You'd think I'm 'on the shelf' the way they're gossiping,"
I complained to my mother. "For God's sake, I'm eighteen. I

wouldn't call that on the shelf, I've hardly had time to look at the shelf let alone be on it."

David had entered my life when I'd just started to date. Nonetheless, my mother made up her mind for me: David was a keeper.

CHAPTER 1

Off the Shelf

It was November 1952, and London was experiencing one of the worst fogs on record. With neither a bus nor a taxi in sight, David walked from St. Thomas Hospital, over Westminster Bridge, hoping to find a tube station. He knew the Thames ran under the bridge, and he could hear it, yet even so close he couldn't see it. He continued on, hoping to find an underground station, eventually arriving nearly an hour later at Leicester Square, having missed Westminster completely.

Finally on the train he relaxed and took a book out of his pocket. Addicted to T.S. Eliot's prose, he was never without a copy of his poetry. I don't know whether he carried it because he related to "The Love Song of J. Alfred Prufrock" or because he, like Eliot, was enthralled with London, its good parts as well as its bad. Every word for him had meaning.

> . . . The yellow fog that rubs its back upon the window-panes,
> The yellow smoke that rubs its muzzle on the window-panes,
> Licked its tongue into the corners of the evening,
> Lingered upon the pools that stand in drains,
> Let fall upon its back the soot that falls from chimneys,
> Slipped by the terrace, made a sudden leap,
> And seeing that it was a soft October night,
> Curled once about the house, and fell asleep. . . .

Tired before he started out, having been on night duty and after a long walk in the fog, not recognizing any landmark, David felt completely disoriented. He wondered whether T.S. Eliot still loved the city as much on a day like this. He read a few more stanzas, his eyelids felt heavy, he closed the book and fell asleep to dream of warmer climes: the gold mine heaps that surrounded Johannesburg and the beaches of Durban beside the warm Indian Ocean. The image morphed to his father's jewelry shop on Von Brandis Street. He saw his father, Sam-the-perfectionist — a loupe held to his one good eye, studying a diamond — and actually heard him say, "Rubbish!" No flawed diamond ever passed Sam's inspection.

David woke with a start. Johannesburg, Sam's jewelry shop, that's where the engagement ring would come from. He could see it, a blue-white stone from the Kimberley diamond mines, set in a modern platinum setting. All he had to do now was to convince the girl of his dreams to accept him and coax his father into supplying the ring.

It was a bit soon, he'd only known her six weeks, yet the moment he set eyes on her, he knew. Surely that only happened in movies and romantic novels — penny 'orribles, Sam called them, like the ones his maiden aunt Becky read. Well, it had happened to him. He decided to propose and then give her time to think about it. He had very little money; as an intern he earned just about enough to live on. His father would oblige; he'd find the perfect stone and get it to him somehow.

David had begun to map out his life on a short train journey starting in the fog, dreaming through the images of Durban beaches and waking with a solution to seal his soon-to-be engagement.

He summoned up the courage to propose on a rainy evening in February. We were walking along the Thames embankment and had stopped to look up at Cleopatra's Needle.

"Be difficult to sew with that," he said.

I laughed. I was attracted to his sense of humor, his impressive knowledge and realized then I didn't want to be with anyone else. Not even Dennis!

"Will you marry me?" He asked.

I gazed over the river, thought about the lousy English weather, looked at him, looked back at the river and said yes.

Later that day, when David asked my dad for my hand in marriage, Dad was not sure he was hearing right. "Speak to my wife," he replied in utter shock, for the moment not remembering his own wife's name.

My mother's prayers had become a reality before her very eyes. What a catch. What a fine young man. So he wasn't a Londoner, not even English, and seven years older than their daughter; but, he was Jewish and a doctor, so what more could they possibly ask for.

Jubilation all 'round, you'd think I'd got myself attached to the Chief Rabbi. Well, maybe not him as he was already married, but certainly to someone of great importance. That was until they learned our intention was to leave London for Johannesburg the day after our marriage.

Tears all 'round. Mother wept, father moped, while my grandparents were sure they would never see me again. My friends thought my decision a bit hasty. The boy next door, his heart broken, retreated to his room; the girl he'd secretly adored since the age of ten was betrothed to a foreign intruder from, of all places, Africa.

Now, my husband-to-be announced, out of the presence of my family, the need for an antenuptial contract — according to South African Roman Dutch law — which spelled out that everything we owned separately was to be equally shared, or if one wanted to keep something for oneself, one stated it now. It was ridiculous as far as I was concerned. I owned nothing. I had about fifty pounds in the bank. Did that mean I had to give him twenty five of it? Is that why he gave me his sweet coupons? We still had ration books — two ounces of sweets a week.

David made arrangements at the School of Tropical Medicine for my injections: yellow fever, typhoid, tuberculosis. He didn't need them, he was born in Africa. He told me he was immune then stated nonchalantly, "I was once diagnosed with the plague."

"Plague!" I shouted in alarm.

"Wrong diagnosis, just had a bad case of the flu."

Soon after, David made the appointment for me and apologized for being unable to accompany me, saying he couldn't get time off. I waited three hours in a cold corridor lined with wooden chairs before my name was called. A nurse holding an oversized syringe stuck the needle into my arm then called for her next victim. On the train home my arm began to swell and my head ached. I landed up in bed for three days, convinced every injection gave me the actual disease. My temperature soared, my muscles went into spasm, I developed a dreadful rash in the most intimate places, and I felt like death.

David showed no sympathy. "Better than getting the actual diseases," he remarked. "Suffer now and you'll live; do without and you might die."

"Are you sure I'm safe now?"

"Well, I suppose we could have included injections for dengue fever, leprosy, scurvy, bilharzia, cholera and probably others, but they're not available yet."

"My dad thinks you are trying to do me in," I said.

"Not at all. I'm trying to keep you alive."

Three months later we were married at the Rembrandt Hotel in Kensington, top hat and tails for the men and long gowns for the ladies. A master of ceremonies, complete with red jacket, white vest, bow tie and black trousers, kept the guests both amused and in check. How more formal could you get?

"Please stand for the National Anthems," the master of ceremonies commanded.

It had been arranged for both national anthems to be played before we sat down for dinner. "God Save the Queen" was to be followed by the South African anthem. No problem with "God Save the Queen," but when the MC called for the South African anthem the band looked aghast. How were they supposed to know the South African anthem? The conductor scratched his head. The guests stood waiting for the music to begin. An eerie silence followed.

Finally, the saxophonist had an idea. He whispered to his musicians, who all nodded in agreement, and played, "Sarie Marais," the song made popular by Eve Boswell, a South African. Unfortunately, it happened to be an Afrikaans folk song sung during the Boer War by prisoners taken by the British and either shot or placed in concentration camps. Could there be anything more inappropriate? Later the MC made his apologies to family and friends, especially those joining us from Johannesburg. They'd come all that way to be reminded of a time in their country's history they wished to remain unspoken and certainly unsung.

Faux pas forgiven, the South Africans wished my parents well, saying, "We know how difficult it must be for you." They sounded like I was being taken off to Wormwood Scrubs prison.

"Not your fault," said my dad, who'd finally found his tongue. "It's him," he said, pointing to David, "all his fault. Anyway, we have our younger daughter. She won't be running away in the near future."

The MC called upon David to speak. "Friends, Romans, countrymen," David began. "Sorry, wrong piece of paper," he fumbled in his pocket and found the right one. "I raise my glass to my beautiful wife, to my newly acquired in-laws, to all of you here today." He went on to apologize for taking his beautiful wife away from them, promising to bring her back or, perhaps, send her back "if the African sun got too much for her." On the other hand, he said the English climate had got a bit too much for him. "We will compromise," he said. "We'll both suffer a little of each other's native climate — though I must admit my dearly beloved is getting a better alternative to the one I've been suffering here."

We stayed that first night at the Savoy Hotel in London, and because the majority of our wedding gifts were checks and since we were leaving the next day, we stayed up most of the night counting money. Twenty-five pounds from Uncle Ephraim, always cheap, a hundred pounds from Aunty Grace, always generous, plus small and large amounts from other relatives — it all added up to a sizeable loot. There were some packaged gifts, but those we left unopened and into the trunk they went. In the early hours of the morning we fell asleep on the sofa — the bed untouched. I remained a virgin bride.

The following morning, arriving at Waterloo Station we faced a very different emotional scene from the one we left the night before at the Rembrandt Hotel. Friends and family all gathered in a somber mood. White handkerchiefs clasped tightly, quiet conversation and many tears. My parents stood, locked arm in arm, alongside the train, my young sister beside them. Aunts, uncles, and grandparents had come to say goodbye.

"You'd think we were off to war instead of our honeymoon," David quipped, trying to lighten the mood.

"That's just it. Wouldn't let her out of our sight during the war and now she's off to Africa," Dad sort of groaned. The man who agonized over Australia, and turned down the opportunity, stood there, perhaps wondering if he had gone to Australia, would he be losing his daughter to an African? He never said it, but I know if he'd had his druthers, he'd have rooted for an Englishman, a son-in-law he could discuss football with and join him every Saturday at the Arsenal football grounds. He'd always wanted a son, and his hopes of his elder daughter providing one were dashed.

My Grandmother — a strong, opinionated woman who hadn't travelled farther than Brighton in her seventy-five years and whose lack of worldliness never interfered with her giving an opinion — spoke up: "Don't pet the lions and keep her away from them Whirling Dervishes."

"Grandma, Dervishes are not from our part of Africa," David assured her.

"Don't matter — I've heard a thing or two about them blackies!"

"Our Africans are Zulus."

"Oh, my Gawd!"

What Grandma's vision of a Zulu might have been, well, I'll never know. She had rarely set eyes on a black man, and she was letting her imagination run wild. Grandpa gave her a gentle poke in the ribs.

And that was it.

The hands of the big station clock were moving toward departure time, and we had to board the train. We climbed on, found our compartment, deposited our luggage then stood in the corridor, hanging out the window.

Mother managed to reach up to give me a final kiss. "Write, darling, as often as you can."

Dad turned away, couldn't bring himself to let me see the tears flowing into his handkerchief.

The guard lowered a green flag. The dividing hour had struck.

"I will, I promise! Bye, everyone, bye!" I shouted, waving as the train slowly chugged its way down the tracks — and my words were blown to the winds.

"Tell me again where I'm going?" I whispered to David, still waving, while tears ran down my face as I realized at that moment I was leaving everyone and everything I'd known all of my life.

"You're going to South Africa with me," he replied reassuringly and held me tight.

"Right, I'm going to South Africa with you." I sobbed, wondering what on earth I was doing on a train leaving London and on my way to Africa with a bloke I hardly knew.

CHAPTER 2

I Can't Turn Back Now

✉

28th June 1954

*Dearest Mummy, Daddy and little sister Gillian,
We have just left Victoria station but I want to
write this letter to you all. First of all to thank you
for giving us such a wonderful wedding reception
. . . to travel half way round the world has always
been my greatest wish — and now that I am about
to do so, it just doesn't seem possible. I shall write
another paragraph to this letter as often as I can
and will post it on our arrival in Durban.*

✉

29th June 1954

*From Calais we managed to get hold of someone
who spoke English, and he directed us on to the
next train. There we managed to get a couchette
and after supper settled down for the night. We
only slept in patches, but that was something*

anyway. We arrived in Basle, Switzerland and there to another train for Milan. We have just left Lucerne, and I am writing this part of the letter as we travel through some of the most beautiful countryside. Lake Lucerne is spread in front of us, and if only the sun would shine, it would be the most perfect picture. Apart from the fact it would probably have been quicker going through China, we are having glimpses of Europe which we would otherwise not have seen. The train is climbing higher and higher up the mountain, and we should soon be going through the St. Gotthard Pass. The higher we get the colder I become, and I am sitting huddled up, trying to keep warm while at the same time keeping pace with the changing Swiss landscape . . . after a little shut eye we were a little more refreshed by the time we reached Milan. Here again we had to change trains, this time to a stifling hot, full carriage.

30th June 1954

On arriving in Venice, David asked whether we could get a taxi and was greeted by guffaws of laughter. There are no roads at all, only canals, so we took a gondola to our hotel. We celebrated with the Venetians the seventh hundredth anniversary of the birth of Marco Polo, while sipping on lemon ice in the Piazza San Marco with the orchestra playing Italian folk songs. At last we got back to the hotel exhausted and ready to flop on our bed and sleep — but that was not to be. The orchestra continued playing, the church bell wouldn't stop, the beds squeaked and finally the clock across the way chimed every quarter of an hour, exactly like they did in the film Genevieve, based on the vintage car race London to Brighton.

1st July 1954

After clearing our luggage and showing our passports we are ushered on to the MV Europa. We are both very taken with the ship and our cabin, though small, just right for two people. I felt a little seasick the first night when we ran into a storm just outside Venice.

2nd July 1954

We docked in Brindisi, our last port of call in Europe. We will not see land again until we reach Port Said on Sunday, although we did actually have a glimpse of Crete today which appeared to be a very small island right in the middle of nowhere. The only feature I could make out with my glasses on was the mountains.

4th July 1954

When one is at sea one loses count of the days, and I have just had to ask someone whether it is Friday or Saturday. It is the latter. We are booked to go to Cairo from Port Said tomorrow. We were advised that if our passports were marked with an Israeli stamp, then there would not be any question of our leaving the ship as the customs officials in Egypt would make our lives a misery. Anyway as neither of us look particularly Semitic and have no Israeli visa everything is okay.

✉

5th July 1954

We left the ship in the afternoon and went by car to Cairo where we stayed the night in a hotel. The next morning, as the sun came up, we were taken by a guide to see the ruins in the land of Goshen just outside Cairo and just as we came into this town standing on the horizon were the seven-thousand-year-old pyramids. At the foot of a long hill we got out of the taxi and went the rest of the way by camel, smelly and spitting, (the camel, not us) not the most pleasant of God's creatures in this land of the bible . . .

After hours of sightseeing we rode back on our respective camels to our waiting taxi, having liberally tipped the camel guide before he allowed us to dismount. After traipsing through the bazaars and Mosques and the Coptic section we were driven to Suez. There our ship waited a long way off shore. First a row boat, then a people basket lowered from the deck. Four at a time we were swung up — I closed my eyes until a deck hand released us once more on to the good ship Europa.

✉

7th July 1954

The weather has now become unbearably hot. For two days it has been one hundred and twenty degrees Fahrenheit. You just can't imagine what it is like. We pour with perspiration all day and find difficulty sleeping at night. The reason for this heat is because we are sailing through the Red Sea which is renowned for its climatic conditions. After Aden, which we reach tomorrow, it ought to get cooler. We have made friends on board and everyone knows we are on our honeymoon. It is now time for me to dress for dinner. I feel as if I'd like to go in my birthday suit, but I hardly think it suitable so I will have to hunt through my wardrobe for something suitable . . . the journey from Aden to our next port of call was just too awful for words. The ship tossed and turned the entire way, we had run into a monsoon, the gusty winds together with choppy seas played havoc with the ship.

This letter to my parents continued, page after page.

We crossed the equator with the usual ceremony, where I was taken by force to the Court of King Neptune and there smothered in cochineal (a red dye), eggs, flour and water and some vile green stuff, and thrown into the swimming pool along with the other no-longer-neophytes. The entire retinue finished up in the pool with us.

Patricia ceremoniously crossing the Equator

After Mogadishu we would be arriving in Mombasa, but not before letting some of the crew off in Zanzibar.

"Zanzibar? Isn't that where Robinson Crusoe landed up with cannibals and mutineers?" I asked.

"No, we are in the Indian Ocean, Crusoe was castaway on a remote island in the Caribbean," my professorial husband replied.

When we docked in Dar Es Salaam I decided not to ask any further geographical questions.

Our greatest difficulty throughout the voyage, in fact, from the time we left London, was currency. We began by changing English pounds into French francs followed by French into Swiss francs, Swiss into Italian lira, Italian lira into Egyptian piaster, Egyptian piaster back into Italian lira, Italian lira into Ethiopian birr and to Dar Es Salaam's East African shillings. What we had left would finally have to be exchanged for South African pounds. We've been given change in Australian pennies, German marks and English threepenny bits. I felt as rich as a king; but, really, when we added it up, I doubted whether it would total a couple of quid.

"Don't use 'quid' in South Africa. I know it means a pound in England, but they won't know what you're talking about," David advised.

I seemed to be using British terms I'd hardly ever used before. Was this my way of imposing my individuality?

On reaching Beira, Portuguese East Africa we refused to change any money. We kept the few coins we had left for souvenirs.

Letter continues . . .

Another twelve hours before sailing into Durban. The ship rolled like mad but it doesn't worry us very much because we know it's the last day. And now we are at the end of our voyage and all that is left for me to do is try to put my thoughts, feelings and ideas in to perspective. We've had the most wonderful honeymoon possible, hardly a cross word, plenty of fun and never a regretted moment. We have travelled on three continents, Europe, Asia and Africa. We have been to France, Sicily, Switzerland, Italy, Egypt, Aden, Ethiopia, East Africa, Portuguese East Africa, (Mozambique) Kenya, Tanganyika and South Africa. It will be a long time before the memory of our honeymoon begins to fade and perhaps it never will. I've been homesick at times and overwhelmed at others.

I woke to the grinding of the ship's engines. "What's that noise?"

"Durban — we're docking in South Africa." David reached out to me. "You are home."

I let that statement pass.

We said goodbye to the friends we'd made on board, promising to keep in touch, and walked down the gangplank to the dock side. There we were met by a friend of David's dad.

"How do you like South Africa?" he asked.

Difficult to answer as I'd only just set foot on his homeland, "From here it looks very nice." I had to say something, even if it did sound inane.

"You're going to love it — not a better place in the world, I can promise you that."

I excused myself to look for a school friend who'd recently settled in Durban. There she was, waiting and waving. She'd also married a South African. I waved back, thrilled to see a recognizable face, I rushed to meet her. Her first words to me were: "I hate it here — he's wearing all my clothes — I want to go home!"

"What are you talking about? You have to be joking."

"No, I'm not," and she broke into tears. "He's . . . " she couldn't get the word out.

"He's a what?"

"He's a . . . a transvestite."

I'd never heard the word let alone understood what it meant. David explained it later.

She, in all innocence, had wed a wealthy, good looking older man who, she found out, preferred her attire to his. "It started when he booked separate cabins on the ship," she said between blowing her nose and wiping her eyes, "and now I have to prove he hasn't consummated our marriage before I can sue for divorce."

"How do you do that?"

"I have an appointment with the gynecologist."

It wasn't the most reassuring introduction to the land of my husband's birth. It was hard to say such a quick hello and goodbye to my distressed friend. I promised to keep in touch.

We were on the last stage of our journey, a train to Johannesburg, there to be met by a welcome committee laden with flowers and waving colorful handkerchiefs. The Royal Family couldn't have had a more enthusiastic reception. This time it was David's aunts and uncles, his school friends and cousins waiting to set eyes on the English girl he'd married. Standing away from them, David's Nanny, Dora, the African woman who nurtured him from his birth through the death of his mother to the day he left for England.

"Unjani? Ninjani?" Dora greeted David, holding her hands together in the form of a prayer.

"Ngisaphila Sisaphila, Dora." David replied.

The prodigal son had returned and brought with him a wife. I got the once over, especially from Dora. Her broad smile assuring I was acceptable. The family hugged and kissed me. David would have to wait his turn.

✉

20th July 1954

Telegram:
Arrived safely. Writing. Pat

Johannesburg was a city with every sign post and every street name written in Afrikaans and English; where *Moeni Spoeg Nie* displayed on the bus translated to "do not spit"; where I soon found out *Fortesueweg* meant Fortescu Road and should not be run together but remain two separate words, as in Fortescue Weg. I observed my father-in-law drank three bottles of whisky a week; had his second wife ask me to speak to my just-met father-in-law to tell him she wanted to have a baby; found out my new aunt Edie never brushed her own hair; learned bowling is the national pastime; watched the women primp for afternoon tea at John Orrs, a department store in the center of the city; and, later realized *hou links* wasn't a golf course. Oh, and everyone called David by his nickname, Buster. Not me. I continued to call him David. And that turned out to be only the beginning of my learning experience.

✉

Johannesburg. 8th August 1954

Let me tell you a bit about "God's own country." The whites live in complete luxury and the blacks in dire poverty. They're the white man's slave from sunrise to sunset, and why they stand for it is quite beyond my understanding. This is how the average home is run. 7 a.m. tea is served in bed, a native woman runs your bath. You have your bath but never bother to wash it out because you are told that is not your job. By now it's nine o' clock, our beds are made, changes of clothes laid out and yesterdays clothes hanging on the washing line or already put away. The Cook serves breakfast at the table in the morning room. Another servant starts to clean the flat, (they all have wooden floors) and all you have to do is put your hat on and take the lift down to the garage where you find your car freshly washed and drive it to where you want to go. For the ladies it is either bowls or tennis or a party held at Mrs. So and So's house. There the whole topic of conversation is their servant trouble or how one of their confirmed enemies acted on the bowling green. These South African women just don't know what hardship is. They have rarely washed a cup, in fact, they don't even bring up their own children, a Nanny does that for them. All they know how to do is give orders and watch them being carried out. To a foreigners' eyes it is immoral and ludicrously unfair and believe me it won't be long before there is a revolution, things just can't go on this way. It is thought the coloured man's intelligence is far below that of the white man's, but then he has had no education and has been exploited all his life. He is not allowed to do skilled labour and, in fact, is a lackey. But could the white man do without him? Not on your life! The time will come, and it should come soon, when all this will change. Perhaps by then we will be home in England where every man has an equal chance to better himself and do with his life what he will.

The position David expected to get at Baragwaneth Hospital had been filled by an Afrikaans doctor who hadn't flown the coop the moment he qualified. Loyalty has its rewards: a higher degree for that particular job wasn't essential. The alternative would be to commit to private practice, which would mean finding rooms and seeking patients — not something David wanted to do. The financially rewarding decision came from an advertisement in the *Rand Daily Mail.*

Without letting on to his relatives, David applied for a position as a medical officer with the Rhodesian Anglo American Company, in a strange-sounding town by the name of Wankie, paying three thousand pounds a year plus accommodation and domestic help.

He received a letter saying they were delighted with his resume and when could he start.

"Should I accept?" he asked.

"Why not?" I replied.

"Doesn't seem to be any reason for hanging around here, I can see you're not particularly thrilled with it, and I can't find a job, so what are we waiting for?"

"Your family?'

"They've done without me for two years, they'll do without me again."

He wrote back to say we would be able to leave Johannesburg in a week, and he'd be pleased to accept the position.

I knew I'd be up for ridicule when I wrote home to tell my friends where we were going. Why would anyone call a town Wankie? I later found out: as a village, it was named after their Chief Hwange long before European settlement. When the young colonials arrived, they anglicized it, probably knowing full well the *double entendre* (a worthless person who wanks; masturbator), would not go unnoticed by the Brits who followed them.

I was more than ready to leave South Africa. I'd been there three months and began to feel trapped — trapped in their way of life, which I found unacceptable. I'd never known so many restrictions, even if they weren't specifically for me. I saw Johannesburg as a beautiful city without a heart. Apartheid ruled and separated us. Green buses for the Natives, red for us; Soweto and Alexandra townships for them, manicured suburbs for us; home any hour for us, curfew for them.

The indigenous population, referred to as Natives, never as Africans, were forced to leave their families to find work in the cities, whereas Europeans — anyone considered white — were free to seek employment wherever they chose. Native children, if they were lucky, were given a rudimentary education while their white counterparts attended good public schools or private ones when affordable. Nothing of any value catered to the African. Separate entrances to shops, separate railway carriages and separate eating areas, separate everything.

I'd heard and seen enough. It was time to move on.

A similar family confrontation to the one I'd recently left at Victoria Station in London came about when we told David's family we were leaving for Southern Rhodesia. His relatives gathered 'round and in one voice announced it was dangerous — no, worse, *suicidal* — to take a young English girl to a country where none of them ever dared set foot. Had he said he was taking his bride to Siberia, he might have received a more enthusiastic reception.

Rhodesia, of all places, recognized as a country for less than sixty years, had only two cities they'd heard of — Salisbury and

Bulawayo — and those couldn't really be considered cities in his family's estimation. Lions and elephants roamed the streets. Dirt roads connected small towns. The government was too lenient. Primitive tribes outnumbered Europeans by a thousand to one.

Where they found that statistic, no one seemed to know, and it was probably wrong anyway. The Brits, eccentrics all of them, moved there just to get away from their lousy climate. And so it continued:

"You have no relatives there."

"You are putting your new wife's life in danger."

"You've been back five minutes. Now you want to leave again?"

And they went on and on, giving us every reason they could think of for staying in Johannesburg.

Had they known David was taking me to a mining town, fifty miles from the Victoria Falls, on the boundaries of a game reserve (they were right about that) where it wasn't unusual to have a couple of giraffe stripping the leaves off the trees and families of baboons raiding the dustbins in broad daylight, they would have locked him away until he came to his senses.

"You know it added to the early death of Cecil Rhodes." Uncle Benny spoke with great authority. It didn't matter that he was a shirt salesmen whose territory happened to be within a twenty mile radius of Johannesburg.

"Rhodes was a sick man when he came to Africa — it probably prolonged his life," David answered.

"He died a young man — didn't make fifty."

"He wouldn't have made thirty had he stayed in England," and that put paid to that discussion.

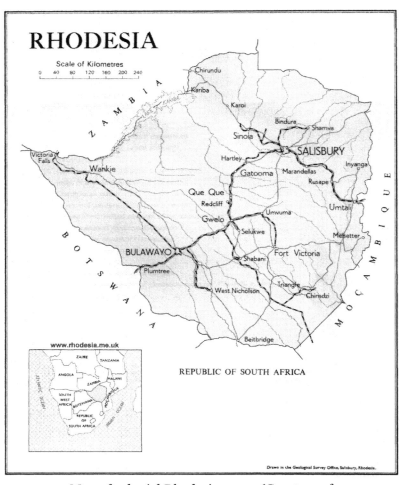

Map of colonial Rhodesia, 1954. (Courtesy of
National Archives, Kew, Richmond, Surrey, UK)

CHAPTER 3

You Can't Take Her There

I looked up Rhodesia in the encyclopedia to see what all the fuss was about.

Queen Victoria granted a royal Charter to the British South Africa Company . . .

Well, I thought, that was very nice of her, since she had never left the shores of England except for plonking herself down in the Isle of Wight after her beloved Albert died, wearing only black and having servants waiting on her every whim. I read on:

The first pioneer column of one hundred and eighty men and five hundred or so from Rhodes' British South African Company left South Africa and established a town called Fort Victoria in 1890.

What else was he going to call his newly conquered bit of territory when his Queen had given him permission to take over what wasn't his or hers in the first place?

These pioneers raised the British flag a little later in Salisbury, and the country was named Rhodesia in Rhodes honor.

A mere sixty years after Rhodes first ventured into the African interior, we were setting out on a similar journey, though this time we wouldn't be the only whites heading for Rhodesia and we weren't bumping along in an ox cart. There were at least two hundred thousand settlers who'd gone before us. Many were British working class, others adventurers, some just like us, wanting to begin a new life in a young, underdeveloped country.

So, off we went again. Father-in-law not happy, hitting the bottle, his wife still barren; Uncle Benny incensed, his wife continuing to make her morning visits to the hairdresser across the road; and, poor Dora in tears. "You bring baby back to me, Master Buster."

Did she mean me or our child yet unborn?

Another train journey, this time overnight, through rugged country, across the Limpopo River, heading for Rhodesia. The train chugged its way through the high veld up to the border town of Louis Trichardt. While it was still light we saw the gold mine dumps and the shanty towns close by. African children waved. Wildlife oblivious to the oncoming train looked up and stayed exactly where they were, causing the driver to pull to a sudden stop and jolting our luggage from the rack onto the floor. Monkeys sat on broken-down carriages pushed off on the sidings; old men begged at every stop; young boys ran alongside the train, giggling and holding out their hands for anything they could get. Nothing to cool us down, and even worse if we opened the window — we tried it once only to be covered in red dust blowing in from the parched land.

We passed African villages where naked children played and mothers fed their babies far too close to the railway tracks. Emaciated cattle searched for food as tick birds sat on their backs looking for their particular form of nourishment. The tiny wash bowl in our carriage ran out of water. We asked for more. There was no more. We wiped the sweat with once white hand towels and longed for the sun to set. And when it did it was cold. We cuddled up on our bunks, hoping for fewer stops and an earlier arrival. It was not to be.

At midnight we were stuck in Beit Bridge — the town on the border of South African and Rhodesia. A knock on the door, tickets, passports . . . we fumbled in our luggage, found them and handed them over. The guard said something in Afrikaans.

"What did he say?"

David, wrapped in a light blanket, answered, "He said you will get your passport back when we change crew."

"Any idea when that might be?"

"Don't worry — the next lot speak English — you'll feel safer then." He returned to his bunk and immediately fell asleep.

I was up for the rest of the night.

In the light of the early morning I saw my first baobab tree — a sight to see — as I stood in the corridor of the train getting my first view at the Rhodesian landscape. I turned to go back in to the compartment just as the train came to a halt.

A guard came walking through.

Baobab tree

"Why are we stopped?" I asked.

"Elephants crossing the railway tracks. It happens all the time," the guard answered.

The only elephants I'd ever seen were in the circus, and here they were, stopping a fast moving train.

"It's why we never get anywhere on time," the guard remarked nonchalantly. "Normal occurrence."

Which, of course, being in the middle of Africa — it had to be.

In the distance there were more baobabs close to a crudely fenced village where children sat in a circle playing some sort of game. There were women with babies strapped on their backs and old men in deep conversation, it seemed, taking no notice of the train or the elephants. I felt as if I might be on the film set of *The African Queen*, except, so far, there had been no sign of a river from the time we crossed the Limpopo.

"Welcome to a better part of Africa," the ticket inspector remarked while inspecting our passports, one South African, the other British. As he returned mine, he added, "You're too white to have been here long. You on holiday?"

"No, we're going to live here."

"Salisbury?"

"No, Wankie."

"Wankie!" His face took on a look of astonishment.

"What's wrong with Wankie?" David inquired.

"Well, perhaps you should see for yourself — I've only been through it on the train, but I believe it deserves its reputation."

Should I ask? Should I wait to see for myself? In for a penny, in for a pound, we were going whatever its reputation. "So, tell us."

"Well, they call it the hell hole of Rhodesia." Then he apologized, "Sorry, perhaps I shouldn't have said that."

David stood up to his full six feet plus and looked the equally tall ticket inspector straight in the eye. "I am a doctor. This is my wife. I will be working there."

"Then I wish you both the best of British luck — you're going to need it," and off he went to annoy the other passengers on the train.

"Maybe your family was right," I ventured.

"Perhaps you should have married the boy next door?" He was annoyed with the ticket inspector and letting it out on me.

"Stop it — we're going to Wankie, and that's it," I said.

Eventually the train pulled into Bulawayo station, where Dr. Charles Delaney, Chief of Medicine, waited. He was surrounded by half a dozen Matabele Natives standing in his shadow and holding *assegais*, slender hardwood spears tipped with iron. Dr. Delaney, who'd obviously had one too many gin and tonics, greeted us warmly. It wasn't exactly the apartheid we'd left in South Africa, but it was colonial in the truest sense.

It didn't take long for me to realize the word colonial could easily be substituted for apartheid. Had I been dressed in a crinoline and David in breeches, we could have just stepped out of the set of *Gone with the Wind*. There we stood, two bedraggled travelers in desperate need of a bath.

Delaney mumbled, "Good to have you on board. Not too long a drive, just a couple of hundred miles down the road and we'll be there."

"Can't we stay overnight, have a bath and have a decent meal?" I begged.

" 'fraid not, can't waste time, got sandwiches, drink, no worry." The man spoke without pronouns. Had he stayed too long in Africa?

What Delaney termed a road turned out to be two strips of melting tar laid out on a winding path cut through the bush. A drunken Irishman, one bewildered Londoner and an expatriate South African climbed into the Land Rover.

Delaney saw my reaction to the mud-splattered vehicle, "No use cleaning it in rainy season, drives through rivers like a charm — gets a good going over if crocodiles don't get you first."

My face must have shown utter panic.

"Just a joke, me lady, only lost a couple of Natives last year, less than previous years. Their fault, though. You'd think they'd know better than to stand waist deep in the Zambezi River and expect to catch a fish."

Ah, one pronoun, and we drove off. About twenty miles or

so into our journey Delaney swerved to avoid an elephant and in his haste stalled the car at the same time, nearly crashing through the windscreen. "You all right back there?" he asked.

Strip road from
Bulawayo to Wankie

"Fine, just fine," David answered, holding on to me, not wanting to admit to being scared out of his mind.

"It's only one of the many hazards driving in Rhodesia. They'll be plenty more. And there were — for trundling along behind the creature Delaney narrowly avoided was a large bull elephant, ears flapping, trunk swaying.

"Blasted pachyderms!" Delaney yelled in his Irish brogue. "They plunder through, don't care what they knock down, trees, telephone poles. I can't tell you how many times we've been cut off from civilization because of them. Wait 'til we come across their poop — that's another problem — can't get 'round it, can't get through it, have to shovel it."

And it wasn't only elephants we came across. Graceful giraffe reached up to feed from tall trees, rhinos scampered, kudu pranced and warthog grazed, all taking little notice of human intrusion on their terrain.

We held on to each other as the vehicle careened its way onward with Delaney singing at the top of his voice, "I'll take you home again, Kathleen," which seemed an inappropriate choice since no one in sight was named Kathleen. Delaney swigged from his hip flask the entire journey and when he wasn't singing kept up a nonstop, one-sided conversation, until he announced, "Got to have a wee — keep the engine running, doctor — you," pointing to me, "how's your water works?"

If he thought for one moment I'd get out to wee in the bush with animals galore and god knows what awaiting me on the ground, he had another "think" coming. "That's okay," I replied, hoping my bladder would hold out 'til we reached our destination.

Eventually Wankie came into view.

"Bit of an eyesore on first sight," Delaney observed. "Have to be honest, when I first set eyes on Wankie, I was ready to turn the car 'round and go back where I came from. Might take a while, but you'll get used to it. Sort of grows on you after a while."

We'd arrived in Wankie, a mining town situated on the edge of a game reserve. Delaney informed us it shared its notoriety with the Rhodesian Railways and The Anglo American Company and had a reputation for having the highest temperatures ever recorded in Southern Rhodesia. "Not a metropolis, as you can see. Now I'll drop you off at the Guest House — temporary accommodations 'til we get you sorted out — I started off there, adequate enough. Oh, I forgot to remind you to drink plenty of water, take salt and malaria tablets and shake out your shoes before you put them on. Tarantulas and scorpions love shoes. Don't ask about the temperature, you'll never get the truth. Mine manager refuses to allow it to be published; no fool that one. Nobody'd come here if it was known. But don't worry, you'll have a fan in your room and, when you get your own huts, you'll have fans.

"Huts? You don't expect us to live in huts?"

"Yes, me dear, we live in huts. Well, not exactly huts, they're called rondavels — getting yours ready for you as we speak." He stopped the car. "Going to leave you in the capable hands of the young housing officer, Hodgeson. He'll show you around. And Doctor David, report for duty at five tomorrow morning. Have to operate early and finish before the heat sets in."

"I'm not a surgeon, Dr. Delaney."

"Neither was I when I first got here. You'll learn the same way I did."

Delaney hadn't exaggerated the temperature. Hell could not have been hotter. When I asked him what it was, he said probably a hundred and something — in the shade, of course. "We try not to talk about the heat in Wankie. There isn't much point, really, which doesn't mean we don't complain. We complain when it rains, we complain when it's dry. You'll get used to it, we all do."

CHAPTER 4

She'll Get Used to It

In London if the temperature reached seventy-five degrees workmen took their shirts off, men loosened their ties and women passed out. No one warned us how hot it could get in Wankie — if they had I might have given it more than a second thought.

Mrs. Lawson, the gray haired, wiry woman who ran the Guest House, greeted us. Her very presence announced the running of a very tight ship.

"You will have your meals here," she advised. "The other guests will join you. Mr. Jonas Brown is in room number one. He's eighty-five years old and a bit barmy. A nice young fellow in room number three, a metallurgist, whatever that is, is here for a month. I have weekly boarders, too. Your room is at the end of the stoop, number five. I live in the PK3 over the road."

PK3? I'd heard Delaney say he was popping off to the PK at the station in Bulawayo — it's what he called a lavatory. Surely she didn't live in three of those!

"Breakfast at seven, lunch at noon, and dinner at six. There's a shower at the back of the house. You'll know when it's occupied, just listen for the water. I provide soap and towels. The houseboy will clean your room. A Native woman comes every day to do your laundry. Put your dirty clothes in the basket provided. A young Native boy sweeps the stoop. The last doctor left his whites with me. If they fit, you can have them."

"A tennis player, no doubt," David assumed.

"White shorts, shirts and socks, what our doctors wear."

No second-hand clothes were offered to me . . . And a PK3 was the type of government housing Mrs. Lawson lived in. Her deceased husband had been a policeman. I gathered they all lived in PK3s.

The Guest House was made up of rooms separated by a flimsy wall that didn't reach up to the ceiling; actually, there was no ceiling, just a large gap between the wall and the corrugated iron roof. A long corridor painted green ran the entire length of the building. A couple of rickety old chairs at one end, a bench with sawed-off logs around it and a ping-pong table made up the décor. My small bedroom in my parent's semi-detached home in the London suburbs was palatial in contrast.

I sat on one of the logs to write home with my typewriter wobbling on the table. I didn't want them to worry so I tried to strike a positive note in my first blue air letter to them from Wankie.

✉

Wankie Colliery Hospital — 27th September 1954

We arrived here yesterday morning to find the town not half as bad as we were given to understand. We have temporary accommodation, more or less to ourselves, except for one elderly gentleman who is seldom here, and servants who do everything in the way of housework, washing, ironing and we eat just across the way at a place the residents called The Lovelorn Arms. The hospital is a stone's throw from our house, well, that's what we're told, but David says he'd have to be an Olympic athlete to throw a stone that far. Apart from the heat everything is lovely, well, not really lovely, let's say different. Yes, my dears, it is really very hot, could be 100 degrees as I write, don't really know as there is no thermometer. I'm told it's likely to get hotter in October . . .

We were incarcerated at the Guest House for three weeks before being rescued by the Colliery Housing Officer. Over dinners I'd learned a lot about metallurgy from Reuben Landau, who stayed in the room next to ours.

"The land is rich in copper and precious stones. Archeologists established iron had been mined here thousands of years ago, and we've found small deposits of gold. It is clear from the evidence of geologists that hematite was commonly mined by early European smelters — it's been found on Iron Age sites."

"Fascinating — I had no idea," David remarked.

"So, why are we stuck in a coal mining town when we could be searching for diamonds and panning for gold?" I asked.

"Because what they need here are doctors, not more prospectors. Anyway, Anglo-America owns most of the land — they don't want outsiders interfering with their operations and claims. You might take a ride up to the Copperbelt sometime. It's what keeps this country going — together with the coal."

Rhodesia wasn't just known for its game parks and immigrant "chancers" — it had a history long before Stanley, Livingstone and Rhodes. Reuben, with his degree in metallurgy, had given us quite an education. I was sad when he left to do further research in the Selukwe area.

A week later John Hodgeson came to help move us into our permanent Wankie home. "We won't need a car to get to where we're going — your place is just a few minutes from here."

I wasn't expecting a lot, but when I saw where we were to be accommodated I thought Delaney, with his weird sense of humor, had bribed Hodgeson to take us to the worst-looking set of huts before he showed us to ours. He hadn't. This was it. We stood in front of two thatched mud huts connected by what Hodgeson called a "breezeway," covered with corrugated iron.

"Here we are," he said. "Welcome to, well, I really don't know what to call it, so, welcome to your new home. A bit primitive but nevertheless adequate. All newcomers start out in something similar. Not too bad once you get used to it."

Sweeping over the corrugated iron were heavy, leafed branches from a very large tree. "I've asked the works department to trim it — so far they've ignored me. It's full of monkeys — cute from afar, a bugger to live with. I'll see what I can do. Don't feed them and don't encourage them or they'll move in with you."

An uneven red-brick path led to the front door. I tripped on one of the bricks and nearly fell flat on my face. Hodgeson caught me. David told me to look where I was going.

"Be careful," Hodgeson warned, "the bricks rise up in the rainy season when there is nothing to hold them down. If we put tar down, it melts. If we try sanding, it washes away. That goes for the road too."

At the Guest House we had lizards and chameleons. Here we had monkeys and, by the look of it, myriad other creatures as well.

Hodgeson pushed the door and it opened. "This is a temporary door — the last occupants took the original one with them when they left. Seems they paid to have it installed, so they had every right to remove it. The colliery has requisitioned one. By the time you move in, you'll have a lock, a key and a proper door."

It's hard to describe my first impressions of our first marital home. Primitive, quaint, never before experienced, remarkable — not in a good way — basic — not in the usual way — and above all, African — in every possible way. Hodgeson must have noticed my reaction because he held my hand while trying to ease my anxiety.

"I wouldn't spend too much time in the breezeway sitting area when the rains come. You won't be able to hear yourself speak, it's noisy as all get out. Your bedroom has a thatch roof. Thatch is better, though it harbors a variety of insects — don't chase the chameleons and lizards away — they'll eat most of them. If you see cracks in the mud, call the Colliery Housing office. Don't ever keep the door open, don't let the monkeys in and watch out for snakes. Now let's have a look around. "

The furniture in the one thatched hut, which was to be our bedroom, consisted of two hospital beds shoved together on a dirt floor. A mosquito net hung from a hook on a bar attached to the thatch. A crude chest of drawers and two soap box side tables completed the decor. I asked if he could find me a mirror.

"Let's have a look in the adjoining hut. You never know what you might find there." It had a sort of barn door — he opened the top half. "Ooops, broken furniture, looks like they've stored it here. I get really mad when they do that." Hodgeson made a note on the clipboard he was carrying. "Not surprising, since the last occupants took the only decent door with them."

"We're not moving in until we have something we can lock from the inside and we're given a key for the outside," David stated in no uncertain terms.

"Keep your hat on — I'm doing the best with what little they give me."

Among the dumped chairs and table, I noticed a mirror. Black patches had bled through it, and it was cracked. "Not that, if you don't mind, get rid of it. It's unlucky to see yourself in a cracked mirror," I said.

"Superstitious, eh?" Hodgeson jumped over the bottom half door and grabbed the mirror. "I'll take it to the servant's quarters when I've finished showing you around. They won't mind the crack. In fact, they'll probably sell it in the compound if they don't keep it for themselves."

I was curious, "What's their accommodation like?"

"Well, there are two separate rooms, each has a bed and a table and they share a shower and a cooking area."

"Not much different to us then," I noted.

"That's right — though theirs is brick built — must have been built after your place."

"We'd be better off there."

"No, you wouldn't. They don't have electricity."

The breezeway, referred to as a "sitting room" by Hodgeson,

had a brick floor, the same bricks used for the pathway out-side — another invitation to break my neck. Two chairs, one of which Rhodes himself may well have sat in, were at each end of the breezeway. You'd need a megaphone to have a decent conversation. Meanwhile, the only light came from a flickering sixty watt lamp. A fan rotated slowly, giving little or no breeze. A magazine stand held early 1940 editions of *Life* magazine. I'd have to find a book store somewhere.

As if reading my mind, Hodgeson piped in, "There's a book store in Bulawayo — they'll send reading material up by train. You'll get the newspaper a day or so late. Now, let's move on to the attached prefab, which houses your dining area, bathroom, a toilet and kitchen. "

"Indoor plumbing, that's a bonus," David sarcastically re-marked. "I suppose we should be grateful for that."

"It's one of the better lodgings," Hodgeson boasted. "Mine's pretty much the same, but I have to share it with a really old woman and her retarded daughter who tries to get into bed with me every night. Might have been a bonus under different circumstances."

I didn't like him. I didn't like the accommodation we'd be given. I didn't like anything about anything. I wanted to pack my bags and go home.

"They don't really expect us to live here?" David complained. "I'm going to have a word with Delaney."

"Won't do any good. This is as good as it gets."

David wasn't getting anywhere with Hodgeson; in fact, I felt an increasing animosity building up. "If my mother-in-law saw where I'd brought her daughter, she'd have a conniption fit, and I'd be had up for abduction."

"Well, she's not likely to pop in, so don't worry about it," Hodgeson nonchalantly replied then added, as if the best were yet to come, "The servant's quarters are at the back. You don't need to be concerned about them, except we don't allow their wives and children to visit or to live there."

"That's not right," I said.

"Yes, it is. You'd have the whole tribe moving in otherwise."

"But . . ." I began in protest.

Hodgeson ignored me and went on to say, "Servants have Thursday and Sunday afternoons off."

I, who'd spent my past just-on twenty years in a semi-detached house in suburban London — even though during the war an incendiary bomb had come through our roof, the windows blasted out and the water from the fire extinguisher ruined our carpets — I still could not believe this was where I'd begin married life. If I saw a daddy-longlegs in my room at home, I'd hide under the bed until my dad came to remove it. Now I'd be living with all manner of creepy crawlies and my dad was thousands of miles away. I had little idea of what to expect after leaving Johannesburg, but it wasn't this. David's digs in London weren't exactly lavish, but I can't believe he looked upon two mud huts and a breezeway one up on what he had there.

Hodgeson had obviously seen similar reactions before. "By the way, you'll have to accept the furnishings until some government or colliery official gets transferred, then you can scramble with the others to appropriate what he leaves. And one other thing, the European mine officials feel superior to government employees and are treated better, and although you look after their medical needs it's not usual to socialize with them. Once a year, Whitechurch, the mine manager, and his awful wife give a garden party. That's about it."

"Where do we buy food? Clothes? Everyday stuff?" I asked.

"Calamas 'everything store,' a shop run by a Greek fellow and his wife, you'll get most of what you need there. Otherwise, it's Bulawayo, two hundred miles south or Livingstone fifty miles north, where most of us go to shop. We do have a post office."

David had heard enough. "Anything else you've forgotten to mention?"

"Let me see. Africans live in the compound. Europeans reside where they choose unless they are employed by the Colonial Service. There are only three working telephones in Wankie. One is in the Native Commissioners Office, another at the police station and the other in the hospital. If you're needed, Doctor, a messenger will be sent 'round with a note."

David walked out with Hodgeson. "How long have you been living here?"

"Too long. Three months, twenty-one weeks and five days to go. Wankie's considered a hardship post. Two year stints, and if you work for the government, then they send you somewhere less debilitating. The benefit? It pays well. If you live through it, you save money. There isn't a thing to spend it on here. I'm lucky. So, I'll be off. Good luck in your new home."

2nd October 1954

. . . there's not much more to tell you other than to let you know Wankie comprises three independent entities, The Rhodesian Railways, The Wankie Coal Mine Company and The Colonial Service. The Hospital is run by nuns. The Mine is run by a consortium in the UK and the railways by a load of drunks, one of whom we are told manages to stay sober enough to drive the train from here to Bulawayo and back once a week. We have been given a grey Vauxhall, filled with petrol which is parked outside. Our Cook is George. Our garden boy is Mkoto. Our house servant is Elias. Between them, they clean, shop and do our laundry. When we need help in the house we just ring the bell and Elias appears. We are told there is always a shortage of water and very often when we turn on the taps nothing comes out. We give it an hour or so, and it begins to spurt, splutter and bring forth a trickle of brown liquid, which takes a bit of time to clear. The bath, though clean, was once white, and occasionally I see glimpses of its original colour.

I demanded the place be thoroughly cleaned and all uninvited rodents and insects set free. I said I would not think of leaving the Guest House until a proper door had been installed and the broken furniture removed. That I preferred the Guest House to what the colliery offered as a private residence had to speak volumes about the residence they thought I'd accept willingly.

We finally moved in three weeks after our initial introduction. My first task was to join the two hospital beds together in what was to be our bedroom in one of the mud huts. I tried pushing them against a wall.

David watched, without me seeing him, until he couldn't hold back his laughter a minute longer.

"What's so funny?"

"There's no way you're going to get anything flat against a wall in a round room. Just leave them where they are. Save your interior decorating skills for when we return to civilization."

"And how long will that be?"

I knew we had committed to two years. Why on earth hadn't I asked a few questions beforehand? Like, do we have a house with a proper roof? Or, are the gardens landscaped? Maybe inquire about shopping and other expected facilities. Was there a psychiatrist or a marriage counselor I could speak with, if need be?

"Begin taking your malaria tablets now." David stood over me, a tin cup of water in one hand a pill in the other. He wasn't moving until I took it.

"Yes, doctor."

I gave up on the beds to concentrate on somewhere to hang my clothes. No cupboard, no wardrobe — I'd have to live out of suitcase for two years!

7th October 1954

*. . . I unpacked what would fit in the chest of draw-
ers. As for the rest, a totally useless trousseau of
dresses, high heeled shoes and smart everyday wear
. . . Had I of known where we'd settle I'd have been
better off shopping at the Army and Navy Surplus
Stores for a Land Army outfit. Everyone I'd met
so far wears khaki or white. Female servants, if
they have jobs, are in nanny uniforms. The native
women we passed on our ride up wore long brightly
coloured toga like sheaths, exposing their breasts!
The men wear whatever they can get their hands
on. No sartorial elegance here, what you've got you
wear. Far more rags than riches.*

In desperation I rang the bell for help. Elias appeared almost
immediately and, although he spoke not a word of English, understood what I needed. He left and a few moments later came
back with a long piece of string and roughly made wire hangers.
He attached one end of the string to a nail in the mud wall and
joined it to another nail immediately opposite. He left again and
came back this time with a long piece of cloth. He tied each end
of the cloth to two of the sticks holding up the thatched roof.
Voilà — or the equivalent in Ndebele, the language he spoke — I
had a place to hang my clothes.

David had no such problem. His dress code was white shirt,
white shorts, white socks and white shoes, supplied clean and
fresh daily. Elias unpacked David's case, took his suits to hang on
a similar setup as mine in the breezeway, came back for his shoes,
motioned they needed polishing and left.

I looked on with envy. It must be something tribal, I thought.
"He obviously likes you more than me," I said to David.

"Don't be ridiculous — he probably knows more about men's clothes than European women's attire."

"All right for you, I've a good mind to send half of this stuff back to England."

"Wouldn't do that, darling, you'd probably arrive home at the same time as it does. Leave it for now. Let's take a ride, try out the car. Do a bit of shopping?"

"Do we know where the grocery shop is?"

"Can't go too far wrong, there's only one road. It's either at one end or the other. If Stanley could find Livingstone in Uji, on the shore of Lake Tanganyika, we should be able to find Calamas."

David, not often short of words, held me in his arms as we both contemplated our surroundings. "If I had known . . . "

I interrupted, putting on a brave face. "How could you have?"

"Do you still love me?"

"Of course I do. Whether it will last out our time in this God forsaken place remains to be seen."

"For better, for worse and all that . . . "

"Better, it ain't, worse, it is. I'm not sure I had this in mind when I said those words. Let's hope we're not tested by the rest of the marriage service any time soon."

"Any part in particular?"

"'In sickness and in health or until death do us part!"

"I'm a doctor — we're covered."

Chapter 5

Can I Go Home? Now?

David was gone before I awoke the next morning. I pushed the mosquito netting aside and made my way to the bathroom. There was a note on the door.

Use cold water tap if you want hot water and hot water tap if you want cold. Cold water plumbing runs along a pipe on top of the corrugated roof hence the hot water. Not sure about the cold one, must be underground. Not sure that you will even get water — if not, ask Elias, he has buckets full in his kia. That's what their accommodations are called. Kias. Tell him to warm it up — they have a fire going most of the time.

See you at lunch,
David

I tried both taps — no water. I put on my robe, opened the door and there was Elias with four buckets of lukewarm water and a small towel.

"For you, Medem, I put them in the bath for you."

"Is there a special time when we have water?" I asked.

"In the bathroom sometimes — in the kitchen many times."

It wasn't his fault, so what could I say other than, "Ngiyabonga," which I'd learned meant "Thank you."

"I bring you water every morning, Medem."

First lesson in bush living with the addition of domestic help: don't take their job away. By the time I got back to the *rondavel*, its posher name, the beds were made, the mosquito net tied up and the dirt floor brushed smooth. All I had to do was find something to wear. I chose a dirndl skirt and a light blouse. As for shoes, high heels were out of the question, it would have to be sandals. Back I went to the dining area, where a rough wooden table with four mismatched chairs awaited.

George, the cook, came out of the kitchen with breakfast: scrambled eggs, toast and tea. "What time Master come back? You want lunch, Medem?" He spoke English. What a relief.

"He said twelve, we'll have lunch at twelve." George hadn't asked what we might like. He seemed totally in charge and I was pleased to leave it that way. In time we could discuss menus. Not that I had any knowledge of cooking; the war put an end to any interest in food, we ate what we got. From the Guest House menus, I knew what I didn't want.

"Oh, no wild boar, no pork and no venison."

"Chicken?"

"Yes, chicken."

"You like dry fish?"

"How do you dry fish?"

"We hang it out with the washing. It dries. Then we make it wet again to cook it."

"Please hang it away from our clothes."

"Yes, Medem, we hang it other end."

"No dried fish. A sandwich will do for lunch."

In the short time I'd been in Wankie I'd read three books, slept most afternoons and had tea at the Mine Club, where women, all fashionably dressed, chattered nonstop about their servant problems. How a Mrs. Jones had stolen Mrs. Brown's cook. Or their houseboy had got their nanny pregnant. None of it was of any interest to me. The only problems I had were monkeys in the tree and lizards in our living quarters. If we went out in the evening, the men played bridge and drank whisky, the women played mahjong and sipped gin and tonics, both getting tipsier by the moment. I didn't play cards, I drank lemonade, knew our servants took care of all domestic chores, and when David got called to the hospital I either went with him or stayed home. I definitely needed something to keep me from going stir crazy. I decided to take a walk, no intended destination, just a walk.

Before I reached the front door, Elias caught up and gave me a hat. Wasn't mine, must have been left from the previous occupant. The last time I wore a hat had to be in school and only then because I had to, velour in winter, panama in summer. Still, I didn't want to appear ungrateful and accepted it. It had to have been made for a much larger head than mine. It's a good thing I had decent-size ears; otherwise, it would have fallen down to my neck.

"You wear hat — too much sun — you very white."

10th October 1954

A few words about conditions in Southern Rhodesia as I see them since we arrived: firstly the natives appear to be treated far better than they are in the Union (South Africa) and therefore seem to be a more peace loving people. They are more tribal and they live in compounds — three quarters of them in Wankie work in the mines where I am told the fatality rate amongst them is very high; the mines here are not safe because they have to work only a couple of hundred feet from the surface and there isn't enough roofing to stand blasting and cutting into seams, hence there are a number of heavy rock falls daily. Nothing much is done about it, I am told, unless a European is killed and then all havoc is let loose. What am I doing in a coal mining area? The last one was when you sent me to that farm in

Derbyshire at the beginning of the war and then dragged me back because I was covered in black soot and had a hole in my knee. Now I'm in another mining area and no one's coming to take me away from it — for two years . . .

I donned the hat and walked out in to the heat — I looked at my watch: it had just turned ten. What more could I find out about this place with such an unfortunate name?

The road, if you could call it that, was sticky under foot. Our huts seemed to be the only residences, although maybe behind the wild scrub there might have been others. The one and only store, Calamas, was where the road ended, so I made that my destination, although George told me he had money for shopping and he knew what to get.

Five minutes into my journey a Land Rover pulled up. A good looking young chap put his head out of the window. "Good morning. You must be the doctor's wife. Can you type?"

Seemed a strange question, I returned the greeting. "Good morning."

"I'm the ANC, Assistant Native Commissioner. Anderson, Thomas Anderson. You haven't answered me. I'll ask you again. Can you type?"

"Yes, I can type."

"Then come to the Native Commissioners Office tomorrow morning. We have a job for you: Clerk of the Court. The Commissioner's going crazy, needs help."

"Clerk of the Court?"

"Yes. You'll find out all about it when you get there. We're up on the kopje," he pointed toward a hill in the distance. "Ten minute walk from where you live. Nothing much else to do around here, may as well earn a few bob and learn what Africa's all about."

Kopje — what's a kopje? Clerk of the Court? Did he think I had a law degree? I'd attended The London School of Journalism, learned typing and shorthand at Pitman's, but none of it had anything to do with the law. The closest I had got to anything resembling law was taking down notes on the Battersea Waterworks submission to build a new facility.

David left before dawn. Having no car or telephone to phone for one, I had little alternative other than to walk. I was told kopje, pronounced "copy," is Afrikaans for a steep hill. A definite understatement, more like a small mountain, it seemed to me. Bands of barefoot Africans passed me on the way up, some even sprinted. I dragged on, finally getting to the top, perspiring profusely — this was not a ten minute journey for a white woman in high heels.

Once a lookout post for marauding tribesmen, the kopje was now where the locals came for a picturesque view of the landscape below. Not exactly a picture postcard you'd want to send home — scrub, coal, machinery, smoke rising from the Native compound, and ant hills like small skyscrapers rising out of the bush. Away from all this, the Mine Manager's opulent home stood out, creating what could only be thought of as an affront to the indigenous population.

The Native Commissioners Office finally came into view: a long, low, government construction topped by a corrugated roof, standing to the right of the lookout point. A Union Jack hung limply on a newly painted pole. Later I found out the pole had to be kept in spotless condition and assigned to it was a Native, who stood every day at the ready with paint brush and a bucket of paint. A walkway ran the length of the building solidly packed with Natives waiting outside four separate doors.

Native Affairs Offices

Getting closer, I could see four doors, each with a placard hung on a shiny brass hook.

LAND DEVELOPMENT OFFICER
ASSISTANT NATIVE COMMISSIONER
NATIVE COMMISSIONER
CLERK OF THE COURT

Outside each door stood a Native messenger in starched khaki uniform, the same uniform I had seen worn by Delaney's attendants when we drove from Bulawayo. There were even more Natives waiting under an enormous jacaranda tree — whole families, with goats and chickens and a cow. How did they get the cow up the kopje? And why the animals?

I felt like an intruder, the only European in sight, until Anderson came out of one of the doors.

"Mrs. Doctor's wife, you made it. I apologize, I don't know your name."

"First or last?"

"Whatever makes you more comfortable."

"Pat. I haven't got used to my last name yet. I've only been married a couple of months."

"Congratulations. Married life suiting you?"

"It was until I came here."

"Oh, you'll get used to it, we all do."

"Have you any idea how many times I've been told that?"

"We have to say it, it's a Wankie imperative — if we didn't none of us would still be here. Anyway, Pat, we mostly refer to each other by our surnames — but that's a male thing. Come, I want you to meet Neville Sherlock. He's taken over from old stiff-upper-lip Marsden, who's been put out to pasture. Sherlock's our new Commissioner, nothing pompous about him, more like one of us."

"You should have told me to wear comfortable shoes. That hill's a killer."

"Sorry, I forgot to mention the climb. No problem, we can arrange transport. As for shoes, you'll need sandals or anything without a heel, and when you venture into the bush with Sherlock you'll need boots. Veldtschooners, they're the best."

He could see I hadn't a clue what he was talking about.

"Oh, that's Afrikaans for bush boots. Their words pop in our vocabulary every now and then. Some Ndbele and Shona too. Not to worry, you'll soon learn. Takes a while, but you'll get used to it. The heat's a bit much, but even that's only unbearable for a few months. And we're cooler up here than you are down there, often five or more degrees."

I followed Anderson to the second door, avoiding Africans seated, standing and squatting all around me. I'd started out fresh and full of energy and arrived sweaty and limp as the flag on the flag pole. A dog barked, the cow mooed and the chatter continued. The squatting Natives looked at me as if I'd just arrived from another planet, although they'd probably have no understanding of any other planet — the one they were on was difficult enough to contend with.

Anderson seemed unaware of my need to catch my breath, to give me a moment to take in all about me. He carried on as if this were a normal everyday occurrence for me. "We try to see as many Natives as we can every day, but there are always more — never get to see them all on the same day. It's always like this, a conveyor belt of humanity. We register them, marry them, teach them, feed them, settle their differences, indict them or set them free. The whole kit and caboodle, soup to nuts. Every little thing requires a certificate or rubber stamp and has to be recorded. It's British red tape and there is nothing we can do about it. Now it's time to meet Neville Sherlock, our Native Commissioner.

Sherlock came to the door — not at all what I expected — younger, taller, shirt tucked into starched khaki shorts, Boy Scout socks in half-calf boots. Nothing to distinguish him from any other office worker I'd so far seen.

"This is the young lady I told you about. Pat, meet Neville Sherlock."

"Well, this is a pleasant surprise — a rose amongst us thorns. Come, looks as if you need a cup of tea."

I detected a slight — was it Somerset? Cornwall? somewhere in the west of England? — sound as he greeted me.

"That would be nice. No one told me I had to climb a mountain to get here."

Sherlock laughed. "Anderson should have picked you up. He'll get a good rollicking from me for that."

Anderson didn't seem at all concerned.

"Picked you up on the road, I hear. Good looking woman like you, I would have done the same myself. Well done, Anderson. Off you go, hundreds of customers outside waiting your attention. What you can't deal with, shove on to Lewis. If he can't sort it out, well, now we have a Clerk of the Court — she can have a go. And send Langes in with tea."

Me? I hadn't been officially employed. I hadn't a clue what they were going on about. I'd dragged myself up a small mountain into a world I never knew existed, and Neville Sherlock was prepared to hand over to me work the more experienced couldn't deal with.

Sherlock, pipe in mouth, sat back in his chair and welcomed me to the Native Affairs Department. He'd been in the Colonial Service for twenty years, felt more African than English, had just been transferred and promoted and knew little about the district he now governed. Before this posting he'd been in the Mashona tribal areas. Here, they were Ndebele, and they had different customs.

"Shona and Ndebele do not get on," he said. "I'd venture to say they loathe and detest each other. Have to separate them in the compounds. We'll learn together. Don't think they're cannibals, so you've nothing to worry about. Good to have you with us."

"Don't you want to know more about me before you employ me?"

"Not necessary. You're young, you're presentable and you're the wife of the new doctor. That's enough for me."

Langes arrived with the tea.

"Langes is our Head Messenger, been with me for some time now, actually from this area originally. He's way ahead of me as far their customs are concerned. The Ndebeles have a reputation as fighters. Works both ways, though. He's fought for me on many an occasion, even came ahead to make sure everything was in order. Call on him any time you need help. Splendid fellow, completely trustworthy."

Langes left, obviously liking what he'd heard, showing it with a wide grin.

"We drink a lot of tea here, cools us down. Learned that in India. India's where I began my colonial service as a young lad. Much prefer Africa."

I thought it time to find out why I was there. "What is it you want me to do, Mr. Sherlock?"

"Start by dropping the mister. As I told you, when they tell me what they expect me to do, it will pretty much be your job description too, except I'm the magistrate here and you will be my assistant. We hold court two days a week: Tuesday for Europeans,

Messenger inspection

Wednesday for the Natives. I prefer to call them Africans, but the rest of the whites — Europeans — refer to them as Natives.

"The Native Affairs Department is responsible for the welfare of Africans living on tribal trust land. In rural areas it offers assistance and legal advice to the European immigrants.

"Native law is very different to European law. We abide by their customs, but if they commit a European offense, like murder, culpable homicide, rape, burglary, et cetera, they're sentenced under British law. You'll be getting cases from the BSAP, that's the British South African Police. They're just down the hill, great bunch of lads, most of them black sheep from titled families sent out here to knock a bit of sense into them. They prepare the lists of offenders and bring them to court. We take over and deal out justice. Well, I hope we do, never know sometimes. Have to make a decision one way or another."

He poured the tea. "And, really, what it comes down to is

whatever turns up on your desk you'll deal with or find someone who can. Think you can manage that?"

"I've never done anything like this before."

"Neither had any of us. You'll learn, just like the rest of us."

"I'm still getting over the shock of landing up in Wankie."

"Me too! Must say it's a bit of a shocker, I agree, but all you have to do is give it the old British try, and I'm sure you'll settle in well with the rest of us."

He was right — the huts were taken care of, David out all day at the hospital, no shops to go to, what was I going to do? I didn't give it second thought. "I will do my best. Thank you for the offer."

"That's good enough. I can assure you it will be an experience you'll never forget. Africa will get into your blood, as it does us all. Sadly, I feel our days are numbered on this continent; we may as well make the most of the time we have left. Mind you, it will be our own fault. We're not all here for the right reasons. There are many who take advantage of the easy living and the cheap labor. Those I give the harshest sentence allowed when they come before me in court. I will not have them bashing their servants or beating their women. I insist the Mine Company pay a decent wage, and I won't allow their European supervisors mistreating Natives who do much of the work. I may not be the most popular bloke in town, but I will be the fairest. Now, finish your tea and we'll take a tour of the other offices."

Along the way I met the Land Development Officer, Hanson, who seemed a nice enough chap. He explained his job: mostly farming and teaching. He said one of his tasks was stopping the Batonka tribesman planting their crops on the banks of the Zambezi, then coming to ask why everything fell into the water when they were ready for harvest. He'd just had the headmen in again, telling them to explain to the people they had to bring the water to the crops, not the crops to the river! They needed an irrigation system, which he was trying to set up. "Not easy — they tell me the pipes look like snakes and frighten the children."

Lionel Lewis, the Assistant Native Commissioner, or ANC,

instructed me on lepers. I was told they were to be kept away from the offices. He pointed out a fenced-in area where they were awaiting transfer to the leper colony in Ngomahuru.

"I have to deal with lepers?"

"Yes, you will be making arrangements with the Rhodesian Railways to provide the isolation compartment, and when there are enough lepers to fill that compartment, you will do the necessary paper work for their repatriation to Ngomahuru. When a mother diagnosed with leprosy comes to you with a young child, you have to separate the child and place the mother in isolation in the fenced area behind our offices. There is always a bit of a scene, but it saves the child from contracting the disease."

"That's awful."

Lewis was nonplussed. He had other work to do, and this one he decided to pass on to me by saying, "Leprosy is in your lap now." He carried on, "You issue situpas on Tuesdays, attend court on court days, and help me when I need it."

"What's a situpa?"

"Anderson will show you."

"Lewis's a pain in the you-know-what, don't take too much notice. Now I'm going to leave you in the good hands of Anderson. I'm chuffed, actually delighted to have you with us. I get tired of these young fellows bellowing at each other. You're certain to add a bit of a change around here and perhaps together we can try to cure Africa of some of its ills — though don't expect miracles. Your desk is right outside my office, come in at any time."

Anderson must have overheard my conversation with Lewis. He was at the typewriter on my desk. "Just making sure your typewriter is in good shape." He fed it a blue form and typed, then pulled it out. "This is your situpa." With a dead-straight face he handed it over to me. "You can fill in the rest."

My situpa

Apart from being classified as a native foreigner on the situpa, I learned I would be receiving twenty-four and sixpence a day, which seemed very generous. Sherlock hadn't mentioned a salary, and I was too dumbfounded to ask.

"Is this for real?" I asked.

"Not really — but the rate of pay is correct. Europeans aren't given situpas, it's part of our initiation ceremony. In actual fact, they're only issued to Natives — just wanted to start you off with a bit of levity. Keep it, you never know, it might come in handy one day," Anderson joked.

"Thanks. It will go in my trunk with all the other useless bits and pieces I've carried over from home."

"Now, now, this is your home, and you're one of a select group of whites with a personal Native document."

"Thank you. You are too kind."

"My pleasure."

I remembered my grandmother once saying, "If you can't beat them, join them." She didn't know what she was referring to at the time, but it seemed to make sense in this situation. I shoved Anderson off what was now my chair, placed the blue form back in the machine to check his entries.

Surname: He had that right

Father's name: He'd left it blank. I typed my dad's name and London street address.

Your street: I typed in my London street address.

Height: He'd judged that correctly.

Chief: I suppose if I had one, it would be the Queen.

Tribe: Brit, yes. Ancient?

"Now, let's carry on with the list of your duties." Anderson started with Native marriages. "They're conducted under the tree outside. Sherlock officiates, you'll be a witness. Court, you know about. It's held in that barn-like building next to us — you attend with Sherlock for both European and Native Court." He pointed out a very large leather-bound book. "This is the daily record book, a sort of diary. Everything that happens here has to be entered into this book. We keep old record books in the safe — take a look when you have time. Let me see . . . oh, animals. We have a lot of them."

"What animals?"

"The animals the Natives drag up here for lobola — lobola means dowry. We've tried to stop them, even suggested going to their villages. They're not having it. They seem to think if we marry them on government land they're covered by our legal system as well as their spiritual gods. Cattle are more acceptable than goats. Goats seem to be preferred to chickens. One goat is worth a dozen chickens. One cow, well that's better than chickens and goats put together. Bet your dad didn't have to trade livestock when you got hitched."

"No but he paid a pretty penny for the reception. Anyway,

why me? Why not the Land Development Officer, and what am I supposed to do with the animals?"

"You have to judge how many chickens, or whatever's on offer, you think the bride is worth. In other words, sit with the groom, the headman and sometimes the Chief and work it out between you. They know what they want — just listen and agree, unless, of course, the bride has already proved she can give birth, then the price goes up, more if it's a boy. That's when the cow comes into the negotiation."

"You're pulling my leg."

"I'm not. I'm useless with lobola — can't recognize a good match from a bad one. Probably why I haven't married yet. I've had husbands bring back livestock and ask for an annulment. I've had fathers complain they've paid too much. Often the woman has to prove she can bear a child, so the child is produced as evidence and more animals are demanded. I've heard the bridegroom say the child isn't his and wants to get rid of the wife and have the lobola returned, and the wife say they've eaten the chickens and the goat's run away. I came here from Umtali, a town in the Manica Province, and that office often looked like a farmyard — it took me days to work out the animal logistics. When I left I made a resolution to pass on the task to a female, if we were lucky enough to have one, and that, in this instance, happens to be you."

"Is there anything else I'm supposed to do?"

"Probably, but this being the Native Commissioners Office, we never know what's going to turn up. So, like the rest of us, be prepared."

I felt as if I'd just joined the Boy Scouts. I'd been in Wankie less than a month and was now officially Clerk of the Court for the district of Wankie in the province of Matabeleland, and David was the surgeon, the diagnostician and the jack of all things medical at the Wankie Colliery Hospital, under the auspices of the Anglo American Corporation. Could it be we were running the country between the two of us?

Before I left the Native Commissioners Office that morning, I received another document in my name.

Ned Sherlock made the presentation. "Not that you're a non-indigenous Native, but you are a non-indigenous European. We decided you had to have your very own copy of a non-indigenous pass. You are now officially in charge of filling out these passes for Natives who come to work in Southern Rhodesia."

My non-indigenous pass with my actual
British wartime ID number: BK AK 99/3

That evening over a strange, barely identifiable plate of vegetables and tough chicken, David and I discussed Neville Sherlock and the Native Affairs Department.

"It really wasn't an interview," I explained, trying to cut up a potato not completely cooked, "It was more — you're hired, no questions asked. It's a strange set up, little offices behind closed doors with lots and lots of Africans waiting to be seen, they call them Natives. The climb up the kopje to the NC's office is brutal. Doesn't seem to worry the Natives, they stride up balancing pots on their heads and babies on their backs. It nearly killed me. Still, they seem a nice bunch of fellows working there, friendly, all Brits. I'll be the only female. That's probably why I got the job, no bloke in his right senses would do it. Anderson will pick me up tomorrow morning at eight, more civilized than the time you're expected to turn up at the hospital."

"What's Anderson's position?"

"Assistant to the ANCs — everyone talks in initials — that's Assistant Native Commissioner."

"So you're C of C?"

"No, for some reason I get the full title: Clerk of the Court."

"I'm impressed."

"Don't be, until I find out if I can do what I'm supposed to."

David was pleased for me. He'd met and treated some of the European mine personnel and knew I'd be far happier working than wasting my time with their wives at morning breakfasts and tea parties.

George came in with dessert — an overflowing bowl of cooked cabbage!

"What's this?"

"It is very good for you, Medem. We eat cabbage all the time."

"You have the cabbage, George. Is there nothing else, something a little sweeter?"

George looked perplexed. He took away the cabbage and returned with yams.

"I suppose you want to know what a yam is," David remarked, tucking into the latest offering.

"I know what a yam is. It's a potato, and it's not meant to be served as a pudding."

"It's not. It's is an underground tuber like a potato, but much bigger, and has an unbeatable, excellent, unique taste. You're in Africa — anything can be served as a pudding in Africa. Most Africans never get a pudding. You're fortunate!"

"Stop lecturing me. I'm not eating it."

"Try it."

"No."

A loud croaking seemed to be coming from the bathroom. "Where's it coming from? I think this place is haunted."

David went to investigate. "Don't touch my yam."

"No chance of that."

He came back almost immediately, "Can't find anything."

I rang the bell, hoping George would come. Instead Elias arrived. David pointed to the bathroom, then to his ears. Moments later, Elias, with a broad look of satisfaction, dangled before us the largest frog either of us had ever seen.

"That's no ordinary frog, not like the ones I've seen in the pond where I used to fish for minnows."

"It's a bullfrog, the grandfather of them all. I bet Elias has it for dinner," David wagered.

"As long as he doesn't serve it up to us, I don't care what he does with it." I sat watching David devour his yam and mine. "I wonder what else is sharing this place with us?"

"You'll find out soon enough."

"Perhaps we should get a cat."

"Wouldn't help. Whatever it is would eat a cat."

"Oh, dear Lord, give me strength to see this through."

12th October 1954

. . . David had to go out to the Native Compound to collect a native person who had contracted pneumonia. I went with him, and by the time we came out of his mud hut, I think every native in the compound had collected round our car to see what was going on. Then, and only then, did I get the true feeling of being a white person amongst blacks. There was a tribal dance going on around the corner, and the drums were beating incessantly. At first I was a little scared — one certainly could not go into native dwellings at night in Jo'burg, but here it was quite okay, and we stayed a while, then drove away quite safely . . . We haven't received any mail from you for the past two weeks probably because it has *to go through the Union (South Africa) and as far as we can tell it seems to be taking five days to get here. The Bulawayo paper arrives a day late and the radio crackles badly, so we don't know what is happening in the world . . . the odd thing is we did hear The Chief Rabbi in London give out a New Year message, and we were happy; it seemed to bring us closer together. I've decided he must have a direct line to God — nothing else on the radio is quite as clear.*

CHAPTER 6

Baboon Tails

A rriving at the NC's office a few days later, I was greeted by a long queue of Natives stretching from one end of the building round to the back and meeting up with the beginning, on its way to making a double line. I sat down at my desk and looked out the window to see them clapping gleefully and performing a little in-place dance while making strange chanting sounds.

What was that all about?

On my desk were a number of dockets sent up from the police and a note from Sherlock saying he would be out for two days at an ndaba near Gwaai and a railway dispute in Dett. I hadn't a clue as to what ndaba meant, or where he was or why. He hadn't mentioned either of these trips the day before. Talk about learning on your feet — or, in my case, on my behind. I had a million questions. Gwaai and Dett I knew, we'd passed them on the way up from Bulawayo. Ndaba?

Langes came in with tea.

"Ndaba? What's that, Langes?"

"Chief and headman meet, the Nkos goes to listen and advise. I go with him, Medem, but today is baboon day, and I stay with you. Master Sherlock give the key of the safe to the ANC. I will get him for you."

He was out the door before I could ask him what he was talking about. I opened the first docket, a rape case. Oh, God. The second, a murder, the third, bestiality — would have to look that one up. What had I got myself into?

I learned Nkos translated to a sort of king or honored leader. Nkosikas — that was me — a respectful addition to a woman's name, like Mrs. or Madam or maybe Queen. Queen? The only throne I had to sit on was a rickety, old, coming-apart Victorian chair in the breezeway.

Anderson arrived with the key. "You will need the cash box. Ndozwi, he's the Head Messenger, he will interpret for you. No more than two Natives allowed in at a time As you see there are a lot of them out there. Most of them holding baboon tails, which we treat as vermin. Baboons spread disease. We're trying to cut down the population, so prove you've killed a baboon by bringing in his tail, and we pay a shilling. Deal with them first."

"Wait a minute — you're telling me I have to collect baboon tails?"

"No, just pay for them. Ndozwi will see to the rest. Come, I'll show you where the safe is." I followed him into Sherlock's office.

"Here's the combination," He handed me a scrap of paper. "Memorize it and then get rid of it. Take out the cash box and put it back when you're finished."

I stared at the contraption before me. It looked as if had come from the Chamber of Horrors in the Tower of London. It was so heavy it had actually dented the floor. I dialed the combination. The door would not budge.

"What's this thing made of?"

"Solid steel, impossible to break in — "

"And impossible to open. You do it."

Anderson obliged then closed it again. "It's a knack. You'll learn. Have another go."

It was the heaviest door I'd ever tried to open. Eventually it yielded. "Hope this isn't a daily exercise. I'll need to take weight lifting classes if it is."

"Good for your muscles, messengers are not allowed near the safe. And, by the way, I'm going with the LDO, Land Development Officer, to the Batonka tribal area. They complain the seeds we've given them have been attacked by evil spirits. They say they don't grow. Obviously, they're doing something wrong. Ndozwi will close the office at noon. Be back by two. Hope you have a good first baboon day." And he was gone.

I soon found out about baboon day. Two by two the Africans came in, one holding a baboon tail, the other there to sign for it. Well, sign wasn't exactly it — an X was placed where a signature was required. As Ndozwi took each tail and threw it out the window, I doled out a shilling. When I ran out of shillings, Ndozwi told the remainder of the queue they would have to come back next week. They left dejected, swinging their baboon tails as they paraded down the kopje.

Ndozwi returned with a bowl of warm water and a bar of carbolic soap. "You wash your hands, Medem. Baboon very dirty animals"

"Have they ever brought in a dead baboon?"

"The Nkos stop them. Can't eat baboon, Nkosikas. People not happy — they get five shilling for whole baboon."

"Did you throw the bodies out the window, too?"

"No, they go to baboon pit."

"And what of the tails we pay for?"

"Some stolen before we collect them — thief gets shilling he brings tails back again — maybe new one, maybe old one."

"That's ridiculous."

Ndozwi had no answer. He was probably in on the scam! "Have you thought of having a messenger gather up the tails as I pay for them?"

"Only five messengers. We have much work to do. I stay with you when you give out shilling. I burn tails when office close. Maybe bad boys try to sell them again. If they smell bad, we know paid for before. Send them away with no money."

I returned the cash box to Sherlock's office, lit a match, burned the scrap of paper with the combination number and came back to my office. On the first day at the NC's I was alone in the office with a pile of dockets on my desk held down by what looked like a dagger. It was actually a blood stained knife with label attached, "Exhibit A": must have been a murder weapon.

Whatever happened to paperweights?

Time to get down to work, I removed the cover from my typewriter to work on the first docket. A twig lay across the top of the keyboard. Strange, I picked it up, it felt soft, sort of spongy and to my horror it began to walk across my hand. I let out a scream, enough to awaken the dead.

Ndozwi ran in followed by two other messengers. "Medem, what is it, Medem?"

I pointed to the floor where the stick was making its way out of the office.

"Not worry, Medem. Stick insect. Prrrrackitaal jork! Boss Sherlock make jorks! I bring you more tea."

Neville Sherlock wasn't going to get away with this sort of thing again. I scrutinized everything on my desk, all seemed in order. I emptied the wastepaper basket, nothing there. I took all the books off the shelf behind me, no surprises. Having made a mess I decided to clear up everything and settle in. The place hadn't been cleaned for months, if ever. Ndozwi was summoned to bring a broom and a bucket of water with washcloths.

The first four hours of my employment in the Native Affairs Department had been an education in more ways than one. The messengers' uniforms were immaculate; the same could not be said for the office.

"If I am going to work here, this place has to be kept clean."

"Yes, Medem."

"Find someone to help you. Remove and scrub clean the fan blades. Empty the wastepaper baskets. Disinfect my typewriter. Get a dustbin to put the tails in. Sweep the floor. Put in new light bulbs where they have burned out. Start in this office, and when Mr. Sherlock returns, I will make sure his office is cleaned out too."

"Yes, Medem. It is time for my meal."

"It's time for mine, too. I'm prepared to wait, so get on with it."

I had to use sign language to instruct the messengers. Langes was not one of them. By the time they'd finished they'd unearthed two dead frogs, a few mislaid tails, umpteen petrified lizards, a snake skin, a walking twig, a number of rainbow-colored spiders, an elephant tusk and numerous what they told me were chungululus, horrible millipedes that curled up tightly into a spiral ball when touched. Added to the wildlife were a few chameleons I hadn't detected because they took on the color of whatever they perched on. I didn't mind them so much.

Ndozwi came back, impatient to close the office. I pointed to the chungululus.

"Nkos likes them."

"Whoever the Nkos is, he or she can have them. Get them out of here."

"The Nkos is Master Sherlock. He, Nkos. You, Nkosikas. The chungululus live with us, Medem . . . I take them out, they come back."

By this time I was more than ready for lunch. Not a car in sight. It was hot, I was hungry, and I didn't feel like walking, even if was all downhill. "It's my lunch hour, Ndozwi, I need a ride home."

"No car, Medem. I make messenger go to the police. They take you."

I sat under the jacaranda tree, hoping the messenger would find me a ride. He came back not more than five minutes later.

"No car, Medem."

At the hottest part of the day, with not a European in sight, I was stuck. The tree dropped its blossoms, creating a purple carpet and a popping noise every time a Native approached. Even the flag-painting messenger had left his post.

Neither animals nor chattering Natives took any notice of me. An elderly man squatted in the middle of small circle he'd drawn in the dirt. He took a collection of old bones from a pouch worn at his waist and threw them into the dirt circle. Two young Natives anxiously waited. The old man spoke, pointing out the direction in which the bones had landed. I hadn't a clue what he was saying, but they were not satisfied with the outcome. Old man tried again, bones fell outside of the circle. From their reaction I gathered that was not a good thing. I'd have to start learning their language.

A woman with a baby at her breast came to sit beside me. Unlike other areas in Wankie, the shade of the tree was open to both races. The white post messenger reappeared, this time with a thermometer. I called him over. The thermometer registered one hundred and four degrees Fahrenheit, and that was in the shade. I was right not to walk.

A policeman on a motorbike came into sight, circled the tree, got off his bike and came over. "Loitering," he said. "Only Natives are allowed to loiter up here, and that's only because we've given up trying to move them."

"I take it you are joking."

"You need a ride. Jump on. I'll have you home in no time. I'm Monty, what's your name?"

I told him.

"So, they left you alone to cope on your first day? Typical, you've got to put your foot down. We don't want you alone up here."

"Well, Neville Sherlock tells me he's also a new arrival, and he's away."

"You're lucky the last NC's moved on. He'd have had you bring sandwiches. We're all glad he's gone, even if he was awarded the OBE. I take it you know what that stands for?"

I shrugged my shoulders, I didn't care, I just wanted to get out of the heat.

"Other Buggers' Efforts. We do the work, and he gets to meet the Queen at Buckingham Palace!"

So many firsts in one day, and now another one, a pillion ride. I held on for dear life as Monty sped down the hill, careened around pathways and finally dropped me off at what was now considered home.

"Want a ride back?" He asked.

"Thanks, but I'll get my husband to run me up. They don't feed him at the hospital, so I know he has to be back soon."

"I suggest you get yourself a driving licence, that way you won't have to wait for anyone. The Clerk of the Court is in charge of issuing all licences for the entire Wankie district. Just write yourself a 'learners,' and you're on your way. When you're ready for the test give me a ring. We'll have you legal in no time."

Monty revved up the engine. "Oh, and just a bit of gossip, the police chief's wife just took the driving test last week. She lost control of the car and knocked over a Native. He got a couple of bruises, she failed."

"Why do I feel like the Queen of Brobdingnag?"

"Gullivers Travels? Read that at Harrow. I'd say because in some way you share or will share similar experiences. You're in a bush town, she on an isolated island, you're in the middle of Africa, she in India. Both happen to be British colonial outposts where it is hotter than hell and everyone seems a bit off. Only difference being one is make believe, the other real."

And with that he revved up, and in a cloud of dust was gone.

15th October 1954

You may think from the stamp on this letter that we are not aware the King is dead; after all it's only been two years since the dear man's demise! Perhaps one day soon the Southern Rhodesian postal authorities will find a way to print a stamp with the new Queen on it. From the stamp on this letter you will have gathered that Wankie will probably be the last place in the entire Commonwealth to get them. Nevertheless what we use is still recognized, and we shall have to wait 'til a new edition is released.

Can you remind me what it is like to feel cold. Ever since we arrived, we've been dripping with perspiration — you just can't imagine the heat. October is known as suicide month here, and I know why. Not quite as bad as it was sailing through the Red Sea where the temperature hit one hundred and thirty degrees — but certainly over a hundred. Even the cold water is piping hot. The colliery has delivered a paraffin fridge but no paraffin. We've ordered a stock from Bulawayo — might be lucky to get it by the end of the week. I suppose when we are back in England complaining about the English winter we might think fondly of the warmth of Africa, but really, this is ridiculous. We change clothes three times a day. I'm grateful I don't have to do the washing. David just came in — headed straight for the bath — I must remind him to use the hot water tap — he'll get burned if he uses the cold one. Everything seems to be topsy-turvy around here.

CHAPTER 7

His Turn — My Turn

My husband finally came back for lunch.
"Want to hear about my morning?" I asked.
"Me first. You won't believe it."

Before I could suggest we toss a coin, he exploded, "The nuns stopped everything in the middle of an operation to bang their heads on the wall to pray! That left me staring at a wide open wound, trying to adjust the anesthetic because we don't have an anesthesiologist. At the same time I'm looking for the offending appendix I'm supposed to remove and the patient bursts a blood vessel, the operating table is covered in blood, the Mother Superior comes in to mop it up and calls me inept. I tell her if her sisters could take it in turn to pray and not disappear without any warning, it would not only be better for me, it could have some effect on the outcome of the operation we were performing. And she had the audacity to reprimand me and say if I worshipped Jesus Christ the way they do, I wouldn't need to ask for help. I informed her the patient is one of her converts and Jesus didn't appear to be helping him, and as I am an atheist, born a Jew, it was little use me praying to Jesus. What did she do? She throws down the mop and joins the nuns kneeling before their saviour."

"What happened to the patient?"
"I think he'll make it."

"Think?"

"I'm sure he'll make it — not so sure about me. I'm an infidel, I'm also interfering with their prayers, so either I become a Roman Catholic or . . . " David couldn't think of an or. "Bet you can't match that."

I thought it best to leave the account of my morning for another time.

26th October 1954 — Stop after hell.

It is said "there is only a piece of tissue paper between Wankie and Hell, and it is scorched on the Wankie side!" The temperatures here for the past few days have been over 105 degrees, and I can assure you that never before have I experienced such heat. From all accounts there is no rain in sight, so we will have to put up with it for some time yet. I work in a temperature of 100 degrees and that is with the fans running and the doors wide open . . . As for the Mau Mau, Mummy darling, they are fifteen hundred miles away, as far as England is from Moscow. The natives here, although far from civilized, are reasonably harmless, and up to now the Europeans have been quite safe. Nevertheless they have many a fight amongst themselves, and David is forever being called out to stitch up stab wounds. Today a man phoned the office to say that he had two boys claiming the same wife and what could we do about it. I suggested they toss for it, but the natives didn't think that was a good idea as they didn't know what to toss — so they are all coming up tomorrow to thrash it out in front of us . . .

You asked if we were eating well — yes, sometimes strange concoction but quite well really. Cook asked me today if I liked baked locusts. He said when the rains come they collect them, and they are delicious. I told him he they would not be my favourite, and he should keep them for his family. By the time I return home, I'll have forgotten everything I ever knew about European cooking — not that I knew much — so start collecting cookery books, and if you find a recipe, you like, save it for me.

A note from your son-in-law.

Well, Chums, the official maximum today was 107.5 degrees and the minimum last night was 90 degrees. Pat's driving is quite ok, except for a tendency to put it into reverse instead of drive, and she often forgets to switch on. She does drive like her folks . . .

much love and save me some snow. King David.

Neville Sherlock marched into court, his black robe flowing over his khaki shorts, his dog, his messenger, his ANC and his Clerk of the Court, me, following closely behind. It was Tuesday, European Court day. Court being a barn-like structure with rough wooden benches set on a dirt floor. Joe Watherley, the accused, stood alone, red faced and obviously defiant, waiting for the proceedings to begin. The defendant, his head wrapped in bandages, sat motionless, no more than three feet away from Watherley.

I wasn't sure where I was supposed to be. Sherlock had told me to be seated where he could see me. Unless he was going blind, I decided I could be seated just about anywhere. I chose to be two rows back from the accused. I didn't like the look of him. Not Sherlock — Watherley, the accused.

A framed photograph of Queen Elizabeth hung from a rusty nail on one of the walls. A dilapidated Union Jack drooped from a shining brass pole.

The Court Messenger, in a very serious tone, roared, "God save the Queen!"

We all stood and then sat again.

Sherlock was now seated at a rough hewn wooden board placed over four unleveled, sawn-off tree trunks. He fumbled for his glasses and nearly had to disrobe to find them. Finally, he took up the gavel, banging it hard enough to knock a spike into a piece of concrete. The court was in session. This seemed to be my clue to hand the docket to the messenger.

The messenger gave the docket to the ANC, and the ANC handed it to Sherlock, who placed his glasses at the end of his nose and read the complaint. I expected everyone to break into a verse of Gilbert and Sullivan's "Behold the Lord High Executioner" from *The Mikado*.

Sherlock stared down at the accused, "Joe Watherley, I read here that you bashed the African, Mgale Matuso, on the head with a coal shovel, causing a large gash, which required fourteen stitches. Somewhat harsh treatment, wouldn't you agree?"

Watherley spoke up in his thick Yorkshire accent. "I was defending myself. He started it."

"How?"

"He answered me back, your honor."

"What did he say?"

"I don't know what he bloody well said, but I could tell he insulted me because the other kaffirs laughed."

"You will not use profane language in the Court, nor will you refer to the defendant as a kaffir." Sherlock was getting red in the face. "Is that what you do in Maltby when someone answers you back?"

"No, sir. Well, sometimes, sir. Depends."

"On what does it depend, Watherley?"

"Could be, if he lives on the wrong side of the street, or his mum's a you-know-what."

"I will refrain from asking you what a 'you-know-what' is. Tell me, does Mgale Matuso live on the wrong side of your street? Have you met his mother?"

Hamersely laughed. "He's a ka—. Sorry, a munt, your honour. Munts don't live where I live."

"A munt?" Sherlock gave Watherley a withering look. "Stand

up and listen very carefully to me. I've told you before, in this court we call Africans Natives or Africans. We do not call them either of the names you invoked."

"That's what we call them down the mine."

With apoplexy setting in, Sherlock boomed, "You're not down the mine, Watherley, you're in my court! You will pay a twenty pound fine. You will apologize to the man you injured. And you will be put in jail if I ever see you standing before me again. Next!"

Watherley left the court in much the same mood he'd entered. *Who the hell did this new magistrate think he was?* He much preferred Marsden — been up before him a couple of times and only got remanded. Good thing the Clerk hadn't looked up his record.

In the 1950s, the Rhodesias attracted a variety of types. Those who just wanted to get away, missionaries of all denominations who felt they had a calling, doctors, nurses, teachers, wildlife enthusiasts, government employees, metallurgists, you name it, plus the likes of Joe Watherley — working class, abused as kids, not old enough to fight in the war and wanting to get away from the industrial cities where they'd been born. Their fathers were miners, working under dreadful conditions, and they were expected to carry on the same tradition.

When Watherley read that The Wankie Coal Company was recruiting miners, he was one of the first to apply. To his surprise the Company paid for him and his family to ship out. They assigned him a house with servants and a job where he didn't have to dig out the coal himself, all he had to do was oversee Africans digging it for him. And when they weren't performing up to his expectations, he walloped them. He couldn't speak their language. He'd never had anyone he could boss around before arriving in Africa; he felt all powerful, and his fists itched to give a bloody good hiding to anyone who he thought deserved it. That's what his dad did to him. That's what he did to them.

"How many more of these thugs do I have to see?" Sherlock inquired.

"Two more," I replied, "plus another requesting the return of lobola."

"They'll have to wait, my dog needs to wee." Sherlock stood. We stood.

The Court Messenger bellowed, "God save the Queen!"

Sherlock marched out, followed by his hound. Five minutes later he was back. All present in court stood again for "God save the Queen!" and the court was once more in session.

The next case was Monty's, the motorbike policeman, who whispered to me before he presented his case. "I think it's ridiculous we have to stand every time Sherlock leaves court. The Queen wouldn't know if we stood or sat, from where she reigns."

Sherlock banged his gavel on the rough desk. "You ready, Sergeant?"

Monty stood. "My defendant has failed to turn up, sir. It's a case of abduction."

"You mean to tell me the defendant has been abducted?"

"No, sir. His wife abducted with their child and returned to Mozambique with him."

"It's out of my jurisdiction anyway — should you see the absentee complainant again, tell him to find a solicitor to represent him in a higher court and remind him to show up and not waste the time of the judicial system as he appears to have wasted yours and mine. I may be new to this district, and I still have a lot to learn, but there is one thing, as your magistrate, I want to make perfectly clear: Be it African law or European law, I intend to carry it out as it is written. I will not countenance any form of violence. I will not close my eyes to taking advantage of any man or woman of any color. I will follow the instructions of Her Majesty's government, and I will treat fairly all those who come before me. I have the patience of a hungry lion and the heart of a faithful hound. I repeat I will not have any of you wasting my time. This is a court of law — we do not mess around with the law."

He took one last look around the court, beckoned me to come up to the bench where he handed the dockets over and made to leave.

"God save the Queen," a solemn messenger's voice resounded through the court.

Sherlock stopped in his tracks. "Make no mistake, I love our Queen. She has my allegiance. But once on entering court and once on leaving is quite sufficient, and if my dog or I have to leave for one reason or another, we do not have to depart with the announcement of God saving the Queen. The Queen will be saved, whether we repeat it or not."

"There's a man after my own heart!" Monty exclaimed.

Back in the office, Ndozwi brought in the inevitable tea. The usual line of Africans waited outside my office, all wanting to speak to the Native Commissioner. After the third one left, Sherlock came out to talk to me.

"Now, I would be obliged if you'd ask them what it is they need to see me about before you show them in. Ndozwi will interpret for you." Sherlock went on, "I find most of the time what they have to say is something quite inconsequential. A European complaining about his mother-in-law . . . now surely you can take care of that. You're married, you have a mother-in-law."

"Actually, I don't. She died before we married."

"Sorry about that . . . I'll deal with bona fide tribal altercations, food allocations, chiefs and headman, kraal differences, and anything you think is in my realm of expertise. The rest is up to you. If you get stuck, call on Anderson, leave the LDO and the other ANC's out of it. From what I can gather from their personalities, they're more likely to shoot the complainant rather than listen, and that would not be a good idea."

I was about to ask him whether he placed the stick insect on my typewriter but held back, deciding the moment wasn't right. I had plenty to do, and Watherley was waiting to pay his fine.

"If your Mister bloody Sherlock ever went down the mine, he'd know what it's like to work in the dark underground. It's no picnic, you know!"

"Twenty pounds, please, Mr. Watherley."

"Twenty quid for bashing a munt? That's bloody highway robbery."

"Twenty pounds, please. I don't make the rules, I just carry them out." I was learning fast.

Watherley handed over the money and, as he left, I heard him muttering under his breath, "She's another one of them kaffir lovers. This bloody government is swarming with them. They'll be ruling us before long, I can see it coming."

"I'll bet you dollars to doughnuts we haven't seen the last of him." Anderson had come in, as Watherley departed, to hand me a batch of papers to type. "By the way, we have two marriages to perform tomorrow, one European, the other Native. Better put on your best bib and tucker. I believe the European bride is nine months pregnant. Sherlock said she was outstanding in pink. She'll probably go straight from here to the delivery room, maybe in time to stop the kid from being bastard!"

"You're an irreverent lot," I said.

"It's humor that keeps us going, if we didn't have that, we'd all land up in Ingutsheni."

"Ingutsheni? I must make a list of words and places you all use, then I won't have to keep asking the where, what and when questions."

"Good idea. Ingutsheni is the lunatic asylum. Another one of your jobs; it's your responsibility to fill in the necessary forms to send the loopy ones there."

"Is there anything I don't have to do?"

"I think we've covered most of them. Not to worry, it will all come clear in time. Oh, there is one more, but you're not expected to attend."

"Dare I ask what that might be?"

"Ritual slaughters. Unless, of course, you want to. They're a bit gruesome, wouldn't advise it."

CHAPTER 8

Ours May Be a Very Short Marriage

My driving lessons were not going well. The car kept stalling, David was a lousy instructor, and I couldn't move the damn thing into the right gear to get it to go up the kopje. I'd get halfway, push down the clutch, shove it into gear, and before I knew it the car was rolling back faster than it ever went up.

David reached over and thrust his foot on to the brake causing, once again, a near death experience. He cursed, I yelled and the car stalled — I got out the car, he demanded I get back. I refused and walked the rest of the way up to the NC's office.

"What's the matter?" Anderson asked, feeling my state of agitation as I slumped, exhausted, at the desk.

"My husband is a monster. I didn't ask, he offered to teach me to drive. Now he's furious with me. I get flustered when the car stalls, and he starts shouting. I left him in the car and walked up the kopje. I'm never getting in the car again with him."

Monty appeared from nowhere. "Husbands should be barred from teaching wives to drive. It causes more divorces than adultery! I'll take over."

A week of Monty's instruction did wonders for me. I filled in the form, giving myself permission to take the test.

Monty, the designated examiner, arrived in the first rainstorm of the season. I got soaked just getting into his police car. He directed me to drive to Calamas so he could buy a pack of cigarettes.

"I can't see through the windscreen."

"Drive! Don't bother with hand signals there won't be anyone on the road."

"Can't we do this tomorrow?"

"It's going to rain for four months. I suggest we carry on today."

We made it to Calamas and back to the office.

"You passed. Make out a licence for yourself. Thanks for the ride."

That was the extent of my driving test.

No more fights with my husband. He bought an old car for me and peace returned to our lives — except for our sleeping arrangements. Making love on a single hospital bed was an accident waiting to happen. He, or I invariably landed up on the dirt floor, which, of course, meant one of us had to go to the bathroom to wash off. By the time the one who'd fallen off got back, the one left was either asleep or not in the mood.

There was nothing Monty could do about that.

George, the cook, continued to serve cabbage as a dessert. Relatives of the first bull frog persisted in their daily routine, serenading us from the bathroom drain pipe. The buzz of cicadas continued from sundown to sun up. And the monkeys whooped it up in the tree.

My life's journey had taken a major turn within a very short time. More challenging than it had ever been for me in London, and that included the Second World War when I had a shelter to hide in. There was nowhere to hide in Wankie.

30th October 1954

The only thing that worries me here are the insects, well, not the only thing, but certainly a major thing. I'd sooner face an elephant or a lion any day. We have huge spiders, scorpions, ants, cockroaches, mosquitoes and although I haven't actually come in contact with all of them yet, I always have that fear that they are looking at me from a corner of the room. Also the place is over-run with lizards. These I am informed are quite harmless and friendly, but as yet I haven't managed to take to them. They have one use and that is they do eat the insects, so perhaps I ought to try and sign a peace pact . . . in case you're interested, the outcome of the two natives claiming the same wife has been solved. The one native was put in jail for luring the other one's wife away. The magistrate hopes that by the time his sentence is up, his affections will have waned a bit. Poor thing he will be suffering unrequited love.

For months it never stopped raining. The rivers flooded and cut us off from civilization for weeks at a time. Mud covered just about everything, which delighted the Natives, for they used it to construct their huts. The Land Development Officer was forever bringing in mud-caked Africans, the Animal husbandry bloke mud-caked creatures. All had to be hosed down before they could be sent back to their kraals — another word I learned, it meant villages.

Cars crashed, trains slid off the rails and tempers flared. The only dry place was down the mine, but even the miners had to come up to face the elements each day, arriving home to angry wives who made them strip before they were allowed into their homes.

The nuns refused umbrellas. "This is God's way of cleansing." The operating room leaked until a tarpaulin was found to place over the roof. The Native Commissioners Office smelled like a pig sty on a bad day. When I complained, Sherlock suggested I cut bars of carbolic soap into pieces and give every Native a gift. I went through a case of soap in a week and put in a requisite for more.

"Enough with the soap, Pat. This is Wankie, not a lavender field in the south of France," Sherlock admonished

I knew the next thing he would say was, "Get used to it," the mantra of the Native Affairs Department.

I stopped complaining about the smell.

◧

31st October 1954

Elephants are knocking down trees. They seem to have little regard for the vegetation unless it's edible. The rain is coming down really heavily. When it rains in this country it does so with a vengeance. Visibility is almost nil and the thunder is deafening. Lightning illuminates the surrounding area for miles around and all in all it is quite a spectacle . . . I have settled down very nicely at work. There are many cases of witchcraft coming up and these are not looked upon very kindly by the magistrate. Until this tampering with the spirits is obliterated, the African will never be what we consider fully civilized . . . It makes me wonder whether it wouldn't have been better to leave them where they were when first the white man came to Africa, that is to let them live under their respective chiefs. Most of the cases come under The Masters and Servants Act which states a native cannot leave his job without permission from his employer — then there's the high rate of divorce among natives married by the various Christian missionaries. They, the natives, always revert to their own customs — that means more than one wife — so what good does it do to convert them to a way of life they neither understand nor respect?

We complained when it was too hot, and we complained when it was too wet. Wankie could never get it right. This was not the best season to be in central Africa.

Ned Sherlock came back from a ndaba out in the district. He was soaking wet, dripping from his shorts up to his hat. "And tomorrow we have to venture out again to bring in lepers one of the mission sisters diagnosed at the Lukosi Clinic. I spoke with your husband, who insists I go with him. 'Fair enough,' I said, 'I'm going to insist his wife comes too.' "

"I can't. I have work to do."

"You will go, and you will drive, I have a bad attack of gout and cannot bear to put my foot down on the floor, let alone a pedal."

"Then we'll drive with David."

"No, out of the question, can't do that. And, anyway, it's against the law to transport lepers in a private vehicle. We'll have to take the Land Rover, four-wheel drive, only government employees allowed to operate government vehicles. So it's you, me and the lepers we bring back for relocation. There won't be room for the good doctor. We'll make a pathway for him and he can follow. You know what they say about Vauxhalls, and I believe that's what he drives: *Vorks* all the way there, and *Vorks* all the way back."

Little use objecting. In Africa survival of the fittest was the motto, and I'd received my marching orders — or, in this case, driving orders. Me, who'd only driven a matter of maybe a mile to Calamas, the grocery shop, had to drive on what Rhodesians called a road and what I considered no more than a hacked out track in the bush.

The next day we set out for Lukosi, a forty mile journey along strip roads rapidly disappearing into the mud. Elephants stood on the wayside. Giraffe peered over tall trees. Soaking wet Natives begged lifts. It was raining nonstop when David, who was following us, burst a tire.

Sherlock said there was nothing he could do, didn't know a dicky bird about cars, and his foot was giving him hell. He suggested I get out and help. Nonplussed, he filled his pipe, lit it and stayed put.

I found David seated comfortably in his car, reading the maintenance book. I started to get in when he called out, "You're already wet, no sense both of us getting soaked. I'll read out loud while you change the tire."

I shouted back, "I don't know anything about changing tires. I'll hold an umbrella over you. You change it."

"Nope, can't do. I'm the doctor, and I'm dressed in white. I cannot arrive at the clinic caked in mud and looking like a drowned rat."

"Then it's all right for the doctor's wife?"

"They won't know you're my wife. I won't tell them." David called out from his dry, sheltered place in the car.

"So, I'm the mechanic, the driver, the secretary and the collector of lepers from the Catholics, but I'm not your wife, is that what you are trying to tell me?" We were heading for a second fight. However, we were stuck — someone had to do it, neither of them would, and there was no one else but me.

Two men, one female, and I had to change the tire.

David called out instructions, I followed and the tire got changed. It looked okay to me.

"You sure the wheel's on tight?" he called out.

I'd have clobbered him there and then, if I could find something heavier than the filthy towel he handed me. I'd taken enough orders for one day, and I'd had enough of both of them.

"I'm very proud of you," David shouted as I climbed back in to the Land Rover.

"Wish I could say the same for you," I responded through the rain.

I drove on in silence. Sherlock slept. I concentrated on what was left of the tar strips and what had brought me to this moment in my short life. Just a few months ago I was a innocent girl living quite happily with Mum and Dad in the suburbs of London. Now look at me: my hair falling down in wet ringlets, my dress torn, my fingernails filthy and the two men accompanying me with not a smudge on their uniforms, blissfully unaware and not particularly appreciative of what I had just accomplished. I wondered whether the Sisters of Mercy, or

Dominicans, whatever they were, would take mercy on me. Probably not, they'd be more concerned about the lepers.

Sherlock woke up suddenly. "If we happen to get stuck in the next river; rather, I should say, before we get stuck at the next river, better aim the vehicle at the shallowest point, put it in to high gear, push hard on the accelerator and hope we get through. If not, we'll don boots. I always equip my transport with boots and push if necessary."

At least he'd said, "We."

"Mustn't put our feet in the water, don't want to get bilharzias, nasty disease, worms crawling out of the skin, really quite disgusting," he muttered, and back to sleep he fell.

No further mishaps occurred *en route*. I forged the river successfully, my heart in my mouth all the way — half hoping David would get stuck and have to get out, vowing I would not help if it happened. I looked back and saw him following in my wake. He made it safely across. If there were ever another war, forget the Land Army, I'd volunteer for the Tank Corps.

On arrival in Lukosi, the sisters took pity on me. While David did his rounds and Sherlock spoke with the Mother Superior, Sister Mary Catherine Augustine Theresa arranged for me to take a bath, washed my clothes, wrapped me in a towel and poured a hot cup of tea.

" 'Tis a dreadful sight that you are." She offered me a crucifix and a missal. It didn't seem to be the right time to refuse. I held it gingerly.

"It won't hurt to take a look at it when you're rested," she said.

My clothes came back washed and ironed an hour later.

"How'd you manage that?"

"The Lord works in mysterious ways, he gives us soap and water and a hot fire to warm the iron. It's a long journey you've had. You'll be staying the night, I hope."

"It comes to something when you need to find a Catholic Leper colony to have comfortable sex in the unexpected luxury of a comfortable, large-enough bed," David remarked in the after-math and glow of satisfaction.

He could have been reciting the Lord's Prayer for all I knew. I was far away in the land of dreams: no muddy rivers, no creepy crawlies, no bombs dropping, just beautiful orange and gold sunsets stretching over glorious beaches. I didn't care about actual reality, all I could see was a cloudless sky and, for just that moment of serenity, no sign of rain.

The next day I walked around the leper colony. What I knew about leprosy I'd read in Bible class in junior school, where I learned it was so terrible that, when found, lepers had to be excluded from the community. No difference in this leper estab-lishment; they too had been excluded. I saw men with stumps for fingers, women without a nose, others hobbling along because their toes had disintegrated. More with sores on their legs and arms, many were blind — a sad, sad sight.

I asked one of the nuns about the disease.

"Read this — it will tell you more than you'll ever want to know," she said as she handed a yellowed page torn from a medical journal.

> "Because of ancient references going back to at least 1350 BCE in Egypt, leprosy is sometimes referred to as the oldest recorded disease or the oldest known disease. In one form or another, leprosy appears to have stalked human beings for millennia, always causing those who suffer from it to be ostracized from their communities and encouraging the belief that sufferers are being punished by the gods."

"Its medical name is Hansen's disease," she said, "though leprosy is how it's commonly referred to. We try our best with the poor souls, but so far there is not much we can do. The only thing we know for sure is that we cannot let newborns stay here, because leprosy is an infectious disease caused by bacteria and the poor darlings would get it for sure."

We left in the early morning, taking with us four leprosy patients who needed to be transferred to the official leper colony at Ngomahuru. I decided I better take the crucifix and the missal along; they might help to hold back the river and stop me from catching leprosy. David had assured me there was no way I could catch it, but then he had also assured me we'd be living in a city in South Africa with all the amenities I would ever need. He went on to say I would have had to have been around leprosy from birth to contract it, and he didn't think there was any of it present at the Royal Free Hospital in the East End of London where I was born. He agreed, however, that bilharzia was a problem, and if ever I had to wade in a river I must wear boots. He left me wondering whether he would actually deign to get out of his car and push with me if the necessity occurred. This time he didn't have the excuse of his precious whites, he could change the moment he got back to Wankie.

Miraculously, the water had receded. Was it the crucifix? Would I seriously have to consider conversion? My dad would drop dead. No, I'd stay with the Hebrew Bible and Moses; he'd done all right, what's more the Red Sea had parted for him all those centuries ago, and it sort of parted for us on the way back.

"Those sisters are remarkable women, selfless and devoted," Sherlock remarked as he came to. "The only problem I have with missionaries is they re-convert the converted."

"They're all Christians, so what does it matter?" I put in.

"It doesn't really, it just makes a bit of a mockery of it all." He added, "On Mondays the Baptists hand out Coca Cola and buns, and the Natives become Baptists. On Tuesday the same lot trot along to another mission get, a Coca Cola and a biscuit, and they become Wesleyans. On Wednesday they find yet another mission where they get a drop of wine and a wafer and, yes, they're Catholics. By the end of the week they don't know what the heck they are and don't particularly care. They're well fed, they don't understand a word of what's been told to them, and they return to their kraals to worship their own gods in the same way they've done for centuries. I only wish they'd leave the rain god out of it for a while."

CHAPTER 9

The Guest List & an Arrival

The expected European wedding ceremony went off without a hitch. A very pregnant lass from Scotland said "I do" to a bloke from Blackpool, England in a mining town in central Africa. What could be more romantic?

Anderson stood in as the best man, and Sherlock performed the rites. I attended with papers to sign as both Clerk of the Court and witness. We opened a bottle of champagne but forgot the glasses, so all present passed the bottle around and took a swig. The bride then eased herself into a Morris Minor and they drove off, not exactly into the sunset, but far more likely to the bar at the Mine Club.

"If she lasts the night without giving birth, I'll eat my hat," Anderson remarked after I called him to make sure I'd filled out the certificate correctly. He left me in a hurry saying he felt sick and would never again drink cheap champagne, especially from a bottle that had probably been in the office for years and never refrigerated.

I can't say the Native marriage later that week went off without a hitch. Chief Wange and fifteen headmen accompanied the groom. Twenty-two chickens, three goats and a mangy cow came with the bride. For some unknown reason they all tried to crowd into my office. I called for Ndozwi, the Head Messenger.

Chickens perched on my desk. Goats munched on any piece

of paper they could find. I raced to retrieve the recently signed copy of the European marriage certificate from the mouth of an oversized Billy goat. The cow wouldn't stop mooing, her udders just about reaching the ground.

"Will someone please milk that cow?"

I shouted for Ndozwi.

He came rushing in.

"Milk the cow," I directed.

"I'll need a bucket."

"Find one."

"I use wastepaper basket."

"Use rain bucket." Oh, my god, now I'm speaking broken English.

"It lots of water, Medem."

"We have enough rainwater, pour it out and find someone to milk that poor cow, since you're obviously not up to it. And while I have you here, I do not require the entire village to be present, just the chief, the parents, the man to be married and the woman who will be his wife — if we ever get down to settling the lobola request."

Ndozwi shooed the unwanted outside.

In my office the privileged few sat on the floor, the bride separated from the groom, all waiting for the proceedings to begin. They'd brought with them a sudza pot, sudza being a porridge-like substance they ate daily much as we eat bread. They took turns dipping into the pot, taking out small amounts and rolling them into little balls before devouring them. I looked on, speechless, intimidated, and unable to keep any sort of order. The assigned interpreter was nowhere to be seen.

Sherlock was in his office making a most important telephone call to the Justice Department in Bulawayo. It wasn't the easiest undertaking to get a telephone call through to anywhere from Wankie and certainly not two hundred miles away. Apart from the other not-so-obvious reasons — electricity blackouts or blown fuses — it was elephants knocking down telephone poles. Today he'd finally succeeded in getting through and now, having made the connection, he couldn't hear his contact on the other end because of the racket going on in my adjoining office. He stood framed in his open door, a giant in khaki, bellowing an edict, which appeared to be addressed to me.

"I give you ten seconds to clear the room. I have a murder case coming up tomorrow — I'm in conference with Justice Beadle about it — and I can't hear a perishing word the man is saying. This is not a banquet hall or a farmyard. Get the whole kit and caboodle outside. NOW!" He slammed the door and the chickens took flight.

All right for him, he wasn't stuck with half a tribe of Africans there to negotiate the terms of a marriage — even though it was supposed to be his job, not mine.

Thankfully, I spotted Ndozwi again from my window and called for help.

He came immediately, removed the cow that'd wandered back to the doorway, ordered everyone outside, caught a couple of chickens as the rest flew the coop, and tied a rope around the goat's neck when it refused to budge. With the help of another messenger, all creatures large and small were turfed out.

It was not a good situation. Not only had they upset Sherlock, they'd also upset each other. I couldn't understand a word they said, but the tone told me all I needed to know.

The Chief and his entourage had walked many miles from their kraal, expecting to be treated, if not with open arms, at the very least with civility. I had to find a way to placate them.

"Perhaps we can move them to the court house."

"Animals not allowed in court house," Ndozwi advised.

"Leave the animals outside."

"Someone steal them."

"Find somewhere away from here before Boss Sherlock comes out with a gun."

The threat worked. Ndozwi rushed over to the where the wedding party had relocated and had an animated conversation with them before coming back to me. "Chief agrees to move to messenger huts. Cannot allow white woman to sign tribal marriage. Nkos Sherlock sign."

"Tell the Chief I am fully aware of that, and once they agree on the lobola and the paperwork is complete, you will ask the Native Commissioner to perform the ceremony." I'd already decided not to ask Sherlock myself, he was not in the best of moods. Better he blows up at Ndozwi.

Out Ndozwi trotted again. No one seemed at all happy. There was much discussion, Ndozwi was trying his best to keep the two sides apart.

He called for help. Two messengers came to his assistance. One corralled the goats, the other tethered the cow, but not before it decided to poop on the verandah outside my window.

"For pity's sake, get that cow out of my sight and clean up her mess." I'd just about had enough. The chickens were returned to the wire cage they'd arrived in. All the animals were accounted for.

But we still had a problem. How many of each did the bride warrant? That took another half hour of haggling. Finally, we came to an agreement. The bride's father would pay the groom's family all the chickens, two goats and the cow.

Sherlock eventually showed up. He asked if they were satisfied with the negotiations. The chief thanked him. The headmen nodded. But a caveat was added and had to be entered into the record book: Should the bride not produce a son in the first year, they would keep the cow and return the wife.

The distaff side said they could keep the chickens and the goat but they wanted the cow back.

Sherlock said they could fight it out amongst themselves, he'd wasted enough time and wasn't about to waste any more.

Ndozwi advised me to return to my office and shut the door. He would deal with the animal issue.

And that was my initiation into more of the strangeness of Africa — in particular, this tribe's nuptial customs and the meaning of lobola: the bartering, the importance of a child, the animals exchanged, the food devoured and, most of all, the fact that the bride could not have been more than sixteen and the groom a lot older.

She looked glum.

He couldn't wait to get away.

The villagers were savagely intent on eating every morsel of sudza in the sudza pot.

Ndozwi interpreted well, but the nuances were missing.

That evening we sat on the well-worn, overstuffed chairs in the breezeway between the two huts, David listening to me going on about the day's happenings at the Native Commissioners Office until I was interrupted by a knock on the door.

A Native orderly had been sent from the hospital.

"Dr. Delaney's on duty," David related wearily.

"We try Dr. Delaney — he there, too asleep," the orderly was saying, "baby — mother in trouble, she need doctor. Sisters want you now at Native Hospital."

"No need for you to come," David said to me. He put on his shoes and ran out the door.

"I'm not staying here alone," I called after him. And with that, I hurried along after him.

A group of perhaps twenty people waited outside the operating room. I presumed it was the husband who greeted us. "Baby take long, Doctor."

His wife had been in labor for hours — not even the witch doctor could work his magic. Sister Catherine had sent the runner to alert David, and she was already there with Delaney, who'd finally awakened enough to administer the anesthetic.

Sister passed the scalpel to David who, not sure about Delaney, made sure the patient was completely under before making the incision.

Sister delved into the cavity and brought out a baby. "Wait, wait, there's another one in there!" Sister Catherine yelled, and out came the second one.

I'd never seen so much blood — it was everywhere. "I think I'm about to faint, I need to sit down," I said weakly.

"You're not going anywhere — get a hold of yourself, girl." Sister Catherine handed me the first child while she cut the cord. "Now take it and wash it," she said, holding the baby upside down and giving it a whack on its backside. "It's alive and healthy. When you're done with it, come back for the other. There are two buckets of water — one's been on the fire, the other not. Add cold water to the hot, should be lukewarm. Find a cloth and wipe the little ones clean, then lay them at the mother's breast. She'll take over from there.

"But she's asleep," I complained.

"Not for long. She'll be awake soon after the doctor has closed up."

"I could do with a whisky," Delaney announced.

"You've had enough for one night," Sister Catherine declared. "Go home, get some sleep and be back here in the morning. I'll not have our patients suffering because of the drink."

To my amazement Delaney left without a word.

No one got the better of Sister Catherine.

A week later the mother came to the Native Commissioners Office to show me her babies, a boy named Shaka, a girl, Mbale.

The same week a near-riot broke out in my office — all over a bride who refused to move to her groom's kraal. The groom demanded she do so immediately. Her father said give her time. The groom drew a knife. Her father said the marriage was over. The groom attacked the father. The bride hid under her father's blanket.

Anderson confiscated the knife, then drove the father to the hospital. Ndozwi wrestled the groom and finally got the better of him. I called the police. Monty arrived with handcuffs and put the groom under arrest, charging him with aggravated assault.

Next thing I know, Ndozwi tells me the bride loves the groom and is prepared to move to his kraal. "Her father, he would not let her go."

"Who are you supposed to believe in a situation like this?" I shouted out the question to anyone who might give me a clue.

"How the hell would I know?" Sherlock answered from his office. "Leave it be. We'll sort it out when the case comes to court."

"I think I stitched that man. Nasty wound," David recalled when I gave him the account of what happened. "Not sure I want you working there; it's dangerous."

"Don't be silly, I finding it fascinating. I'm surprised at you — born in Africa, spent most of your life in Africa — and yet you're unaware of this sort of thing going on."

"That's not so, I saw many a Native before I qualified. You don't spend four years working at Baragwaneth Hospital without learning something about them. I agree most Europeans have little interest, actually don't care what happens outside their comfortable surroundings. They don't go into the townships. They have nothing to do with Natives unless they employ them. Apart from the obvious perks, they could be living in any big city anywhere in the world. I might not know their customs, but I do know their diseases, and I've stitched up enough Natives to know knives are the choice of weapon, and they use them indiscriminately."

"Well they're all missing out. I wouldn't want to live this way forever, but I'm glad to be where I am, doing what I do."

"You were ready to pack your bags and leave just a short time ago."

"Not now. I'm where I want to be, with you, in the bush, in Africa."

The moment was about to turn romantic when there was a knock on the door. At this hour, it must be a medical emergency. David went to the door.

It was Ndozwi. "Unyoko Umama on the phone, want to speak to Nkosikas."

CHAPTER 10

A Telephone Call

We jumped in the car, drove up to the NC's office, rushed to the phone being held by Sherlock, who was having an animated conversation with a woman he'd obviously never met. Whatever was being said on the other end of the telephone in London couldn't have been that bad because Sherlock appeared not in the least concerned.

"And when I visit London I'd love to have dinner with you . . . ah, they have arrived, lovely chatting with you. I'll pass you over to your lovely daughter."

I grabbed the receiver, realizing now who was on the other end of the line. "What is it, Mummy? Are you all right? Daddy?"

"Daddy and I have just finished breakfast and having a cup of tea. He's holding up the paper for me to read the headlines, in fact, a blind man could probably make out the headlines they are so large: Mau Mau Attack White Farmers. You said when you left London you'd be in a modern city. Well, when I read your letters, you're in anything but, and that's worrying. Daddy is beside himself, actually I don't let him read your letters — I read them to him, leaving out some of the more lurid details. He'd have a nervous breakdown if he knew what his little girl is up to. Now, darling, don't misunderstand, they are most interesting and keep sending them, but do please watch out for the Natives. From what

I read in the paper, I get the feeling they don't want us any-where in Africa."

"Mummy, I've told you we're fine, we're nowhere near the Mau Mau or the Kikuyu — they're in Kenya. Find an atlas — there's one in the bookcase — you'll see the distance between Rhodesia and Kenya. And the Natives I work with want us here. We do good work."

"But, darling, anywhere in Africa is dangerous, and, from the sound of it, you're in a place with very few Europeans and millions of black people. Daddy agrees with me — you must come home."

Knowing my dad, he hadn't any choice; it was far easier to agree with his wife than have a political discussion. I assured my mother we weren't under any threat from the Natives and that I hadn't been bludgeoned or raped or knifed. What I refrained from telling her was what it was we had to do just to get to a telephone. Little did she know it was far more dangerous to leave home in the dark, move two baboons sitting on the bonnet of the car, drive up the kopje with no street lights just to answer a telephone ringing in the Native Commissioners Office. Add to this nocturnal wildlife searching their prey and the time close to midnight, and she would well have been on the next plane out to drag me back.

"It's an adventure, Mummy, and tomorrow we're going to the Victoria Falls."

"That's lovely. Have a word with Da —" the line cut off in mid-sentence. Poor Dad, even on a long distance call, he couldn't get a word in.

"Your mother should only know an elephant probably knocked down a telephone pole," David joked.

"What she doesn't know won't worry her," Sherlock assured. "Now come back to my place. We'll have a night cap together."

"It's a bit late," I said, hoping he'd agree.

"It's Rhodesia, my girl. You should have learned by now it's never too early or too late for libation. When the sun goes down we raise our glass. When the sun comes up we look forward to it going down again. So tonight we'll have a sundowner together, even if it is pitch black outside and long past sundown."

Over drinks I asked whether I could take Friday off. David planned to inspect a clinic off the Falls Road and from there we could go on to the Victoria Falls for the weekend.

"No problem, we'll manage without you for a day." Somewhat in his cups and grateful for the company, he lapsed into a nostalgic mood. "I envy you your first sight of the falls. It's a marvel of nature, magnificent sight to behold. I'll never forget my first sighting, left me quite breathless. Pity the old Queen, for whom they were named, never laid eyes on it. Mind you, she wasn't exactly an intrepid traveler, though I must say she managed to send emissaries around the Empire with excellent results. Or perhaps I should say the ever-decreasing Empire."

He offered to fill our glasses.

I declined.

"You'll never become one of us if you don't learn a little of what you fancy does you good."

" 'fraid won't do me much good. I have an adverse reaction to alcohol."

"Pity."

CHAPTER 11

Time Off from Wankie

The breathtaking landscape of Rhodesia had little going for it in Wankie, with its mining rigs, coal dumps and combustible slag heaps. However, from the top of the kopje looking north, on a clear day you could see the strip road that promised a way to escape from the ever present reminder that you were living in a mining town.

We took the Falls Road, driving through the bush past Native villages, over ragged black tar strips — some melted, others broken or disappeared completely —and wound our way to the clinic before going on to the Victoria Falls. We crossed a makeshift construction over the Matetsi River: a bridge with no sides, made up of lengths of loose planks on flimsy wooden stilts. We'd been told not to look down, not to look sideways, just to hold on to the driving wheel, aim straight and pray we'd get to the other side without falling into the river below.

We made it over the Matesi Bridge and a couple of miles later turned off the strip road to a dirt pathway, heading to the clinic close to a nearby kraal. Outside a government building, similar to the Native Commissioners Office but much smaller, there had to be fifty or more Natives waiting. An African woman in a blue uniform came to greet us.

"We welcome you, Doctor. We need you, Doctor." She led us past the waiting crowds to a small windowless room, sparsely furnished with a desk, a chair, and a table with a blanket over it.

"Is there no light?" David asked.

"No electricity, Doctor."

I ran back to the car to get a torch then held it over each patient as David examined them.

"This is scurvy," he told the attending African nurse and the mother, holding a crying baby covered in sores. "Clean the sores, and give her vitamin C. Next."

"Look, Sister," David drew the nurse's attention to the man he'd examined, "this is a typical case of Yaws. It starts with a single lesion and spreads to the skin of the face, hands, feet and genitals. He has to be placed in isolation — Yaws spreads like wildfire. If you don't isolate this man, you will have an epidemic on your hands. He needs a shot of penicillin. Give the mother a shot and any other case you come across."

In an hour he had seen close to fifty patients with a variety of diseases. Many with vitamin deficiency, others with infected sores, quite a few with malaria symptoms. I saw my first case of elephantiasis — an older woman, her legs and ankles so swollen she had to be carried in on a stretcher made out of bamboo sticks and an old bed sheet.

"What would they have done without us — you?" I said to David as we departed, waving to the nurse and her patients.

"What they did before we came? Use witch doctors. Some of their remedies worked, but it's penicillin that's kept many of them alive today. Malaria is still a killer. We need to educate them. We hand out pills, but so few take them."

"Those poor children . . . "

We drove on in silence — I thought I'd seen it all where I worked. I hadn't.

David broke the silence. "I did a year of tropical medicine in medical school. Never thought I'd need it, but here it has certainly come in handy. I had highfalutin' ideas then: must get the membership of the Royal College in England, must get out of Africa, must set up a posh practice. And here I am, back in Africa, practicing what I thought I'd never have to use."

"They need you."

"I suppose they do."

Back on the strip road we drove on. Giraffe and baboons, warthog and rhinos, staring, sometimes stopping us. The occasional car came from the opposite direction. David made room for it to pass by easing our car onto a single strip, then carefully maneuvering it back to the two. Soon we heard the rush of falling water.

"I hear it! I hear it! Sounds like a thundering herd!" I exclaimed as I poked my head out of the window. "It must be the Victoria Falls."

We parked the car and walked the pathway covered by dripping trees that led to the amazing expanse of the raging Victoria Falls. Confounding in its immensity, the Zambezi River cascaded hundreds of feet into a long, deep ravine. Double rainbows arched over white meringue-like liquid sculptures.

We were soaked by the mist, and we didn't care. We had never ever seen anything quite so magnificent, so dramatic in all our born days. We stood beneath the statue of Livingstone overlooking the falls.

"It's hard to imagine what he must have felt when he first laid eyes on all this." David had done his homework. He handed me a book opened at the page he wanted me to read. It was what Stanley had written:

I pushed back the crowds, and, passing from the rear, walked down a living avenue of people until I came in front of the semicircle of Arabs, in the front of which stood the white man with the gray beard. As I advanced slowly toward him I noticed he was pale, looked wearied, had a gray beard, wore a bluish cap with a faded gold band round it, had on a red-sleeved waistcoat and a pair of gray tweed trousers. I would have run to him, only I was a coward in the presence of such a mob, — would have embraced him, only, he being an Englishman, I did not know how he would receive me; so I did what cowardice and false pride suggested was the best thing, — walked deliberately to him,"

—Dr. David Livingstone 15th February, 1856

"They didn't meet at the Victoria Falls, though, they met on the shores of Lake Tanganyika. And whether Stanley said, 'Dr. Livingstone, I presume,' could well be apocryphal — some say humorous. After all, he was the only other white person for hundreds of miles. When Livingstone died, the tribe that attended him removed his heart and buried it where they said he belonged, in Africa. His body made the long journey back to England to be interred in Westminster Abbey."

It was not unusual for David to be teaching me something. Marrying so young had taken me away from my studies at the School of Journalism. David had become, in many ways, my mentor and my professor.

The Victoria Falls

7th November 1954

We've just returned from the Victoria Falls and as on most of our trips we had a few incidents starting with baboons and ending in a rewarding view of the magnificent Falls. On our way back we had to go through a diversion and somehow or other we missed the road and just seemed to be going for miles along a very poor track. The rain was coming down really heavily now and added to that we could hear the Falls in the distance and it made everything sound worse. To cut a long story short we got stuck in the mud and try as we may we just couldn't move the car, the back wheels kept revving round but still couldn't get a grip. We tried putting straw and stones under the back wheels, but it just didn't seem to help. By this time it was 5.30 pm and in less than an hour it would be dark so we decided to abandon the car and walk to the nearest European house which could have been miles and miles away. We were in a shocking state, covered in mud. We locked up the car, put on the side lights and started off. My poor old sandals were in such a state by this time that I just took them off and went bare footed, even the creepy crawlies didn't worry me. All I wanted was to find a bed for the night. We walked on through the mud with no sign of human life. After what seemed like forever we met a native and asked him where the White Boss lived. He pointed in the opposite direction from where we'd come from. We walked and walked and came across a kraal. There one of the boys offered to take us to the nearest farm house. He carried my shoes and led the way. The owners welcomed us and said it would be impossible to try and get the car out that night so we slept at the farmhouse. Early this morning David and Mr. Campbell, the farmer, went along in a vanette to dig out the car and with the help of six natives they managed to dislodge it. We made our adieus and carried on to The Fall . . . double rainbows hung over heavy tumbling reflecting liquid sheets. A white cloud of spray lifted its way to the now clear blue sky. Water rushed over rocky crevices on their suicidal journey. An unending vista of white, white water that roars as it plunges in to the Zambezi River far below. For a distance of a mile this amazing panorama repeats and repeats, from the rapids above to the cavernous depths of the hidden cataracts. Perpetual motion in an awesome setting. We are so close, we walk the pathways, a bridge comes in to view, it is the bridge that separates the two Rhodesias. . . . The natives call The Falls Mosi-o-tunya which means 'the smoke that thunders.' This is the beginning of the rainy season, the Zambezi is at its lowest ebb and I'm told the Falls are not at their best — I find it hard to imagine what it must be like when the River is in full flood — we will go again in a couple of months and see. In the meantime I attach a picture of the Nyaminyami. The Nyaminyami is the Zambezi river god. There have been many sightings of this river god by the local tribesmen — probably just another croc — but they believe he, or maybe she, is not a good god; he causes 'maningi' (many) problems and every time any river, not just the Zambezi, floods, the indigenous people blame it on the Nyaminyami.

Nyaminyami

Please send me another pair of sandals, I'm feeding mine to the crocodiles and the Nyaminyami can have a morsel, too.

CHAPTER 12

I'm Getting Used to It

I 'd settled well into my duties as Clerk of the Court. The young officers gave up their practical jokes. There were no more horrendous insects under my typewriter cover, no more large animals waiting for me in the courtroom. Ned Sherlock was my friend as well as my boss. Anderson spent more time out of the office than in because he knew I was capable of carrying out the work consigned to him. The messengers, who were at first wary of a woman in a European man's job, couldn't do enough for me, and it wasn't unusual for the Natives to bypass the old staff and meet with me directly. Getting involved in trivia took too much of my time, but what could I do? They recognized a softy when they saw one, and none of the NC's could ever be placed in that category.

The Native women brought their new-born babies, their uncles, their aunts — in fact, anyone they would like me to meet. I was the Clerk of the Court, the right hand of the Native Commissioner, the sympathetic listener and more a suntanned Rhodesian than the peaches-and-cream Londoner who first stepped foot on Rhodesian soil. I could even manage to walk up the kopje without feeling out of breath by the time I reached the top.

David worked hard to get his medical degree in South Africa, gone to London to take the membership of the Royal College of Physicians, decided on cardiology as his specialty and now found himself practicing medicine in the bush. Africans rarely suffered from heart problems; they didn't live long enough to get heart disease, he told me.

What my husband hadn't factored in when he accepted the position here in Wankie was the problem he was having with Delaney, his superior, who was either drunk or sleeping off a hangover. The last two medical officers had given up, they weren't about to take the consequences for Delaney's mistakes.

David's duties included all medical challenges, from obstetrics to tuberculosis, from leprosy to sore throats, and now he had another: forensic pathologist in a murder case. The latter being the reason for his court appearance that day. He needed to get it over as quickly as possible because Delaney was once again indisposed and the nuns were having a fit.

The victim was a young African male who'd been found hanging from a tree. The condition of the body proved he'd been long dead before being strung up. In my capacity of court reporter, I took down in shorthand every word my husband uttered. I hoped he wouldn't go into the gory details, but on further questioning he was asked to give a full account of the state of the body when he first saw it.

"The death had taken place earlier than the hanging," David stated. "It wasn't a difficult assumption to make — there were knife wounds and puncture marks all over the body. You don't have to have a medical degree to come to that conclusion. And, what's more, it was most likely a ritual, sacrificial murder because various organs, including the testicles, had been removed."

Sherlock asked the prosecutor what evidence he had to apprehend the accused.

"The body was brought in by one of the village elders who found it at the entrance to their kraal. We know there is bad blood between these two kraals. The headman said the dead man, who belonged in their kraal, raped one of their women in the other kraal, and that, he believed, could well be the reason for the killing."

When asked whether the woman in question was present

in court, John Dickens, a good looking, newly arrived young trooper answered, "She is nowhere to be found. I've visited both kraals, and, so far, she has eluded me."

"Eluded? What you should say, young man, is you haven't completed your investigation. You have a body, you think you have a suspect, and now you tell me you can't find the only witness who can identify the accused."

"I've been here a week, sir."

"I don't care if you've been here a year — don't bring a case to my court without an iota of concrete evidence."

Anderson, in charge of Sherlock's dog, whispered to Monty, "That's what happens when you put a greenhorn on the case. What the fuck do they think they're doing?"

"Anderson, remove yourself and my dog from this court."

We waited for them to leave, Sherlock tapping his finger on the bench until they were gone . . . me, with pen poised for further evidence.

"I suppose . . . " Dickens got no further.

"In this court we do not suppose, Trooper Dickens. We either know or we don't know. We deal with facts. There is only one fact: we have a body with missing parts — the rest is either hearsay or revenge. Supposition is not valid. I am remanding the accused into custody until such time as you find the woman who was raped. Go back, question every member of both kraals and come to me with some viable explanation and not a load of poppycock hearsay. I give permission for the body to be buried. Doctor, you can return to treating the sick. And a word of advice to you, Monty. I will have no whispering in my court. If you have something to say, say it out loud."

Sherlock called me to the bench. "Do not, I repeat, do not enter into the record anything of what I have said in my reply to Trooper Dickens, that's personal."

We all stood.

"God save the Queen."

Sherlock marched out in a foul mood.

The defendant was led away.

I'd reached the last page in my notebook and felt the usual

panic, hoping the evidence I'd taken down in shorthand would not be too difficult to decipher. Whether the defendant actually committed the crime was questionable. He certainly couldn't have done it alone. So, who in his kraal helped him? That's what Dickens had to find out.

Sherlock hadn't for one moment expected him to come up with the answer, but he should have been able to locate the woman. In the meantime, the accused was put away for his own safety in a cell at the police station. The case, as far as our involvement was concerned, would be sent down to Bulawayo to be heard in the Matabeleland High Court. Sherlock, a district magistrate, had limited power.

There were many family feuds among the Ndebele tribes and fights were not uncommon in the Native compound. Becoming a Christian did not erase their belief in the spirits who'd guided them long before the white man stepped foot in Africa. The demands of the spirits still had to be satisfied: Witch doctors, Sangomas, threw bones. Mhondoros, respected spiritual guardians, made potions. Bloodletting continued and both humans and animals were sacrificed. District and Native Commissioners could do little to stop them.

Dickens and I had much in common. We were about the same age, came from the suburbs of London and were learning on the job. Sherlock had given him a rough time, and his fellow troopers seemed to be testing him. I felt he needed my support. "I suppose it's a bit like being a new student in Oxford or Cambridge. You're put through a sort of initiation, although it will probably be worse for you here than it was for me. I think they held back a bit because I'm the only girl. In the end, it's worth it. Don't let it get to you."

Monty came to Dickens' defense; he'd been through what the young constable experienced and joined him in the investigation. Lips were sealed in both kraals. They eventually found the woman held captive in another kraal guarded by a number of older women. She told them what happened: she wasn't raped — she had sex with the accused while promised to another man.

"So what now?" I asked Monty when they came back. "Why isn't she with you?"

"The Chief's in charge of her punishment, nothing to do with us."

"And the poor bugger we've got locked up?"

"He'll be set free eventually. Up to him whether he dares to go back to his kraal. If I were him, I'd scarper. They're a vicious lot when it comes to breaking custom, and if it involves a woman promised to another, God help you."

The ritual murder had not been solved so I kept the docket open. What people did to each other, be they black or white, left me little hope for the future of a less violent Africa. Native murderers found numerous ways of ending the life of someone who had done them wrong. They'd cast a spell, slaughter their wife, poison their husband, knife an adulterer, set fire to a village, set traps — to mention just a few of their favorite methods.

The accused in one case said if he'd known the man he killed had been diagnosed with a heart problem, he'd have waited for the bastard to die.

Sherlock heartily agreed with him. "Timing is everything," he said as he ordered a similar case to be sent to Bulawayo to be tried in the High Court, then banged his gavel on the bench, thus calling for the next "whatever."

Europeans seemed to value life a little more, though there were a few charges of culpable homicide, which I finally understood meant, though the victim was dead, it was not the assailant's intent to kill him. Other crimes, not uncommon and equally divided between the two races, were deadly assault, drunk driving, fraud and heated disagreements that ended in some dreadful injury, for which the injured requested compensation.

There were times when Sherlock and I were the only two Europeans in the room — well, it wasn't exactly a room, more like a leaking barn. Many a day I sat under an umbrella held by one of the messengers while the ink from the pen blurred the words seeping into wet paper as I tried to take down the evidence in shorthand. Transcribing my notes in the rainy season certainly had its drawbacks. If the blotched sentence had become completely unreadable, I wrote what I could recall from memory.

✉

29th November 1954

Yesterday we went out shooting — miles away from civilization — not that there's much of that around here, the N C said I needed to know how to use a gun for my own protection. We fixed up a broken sign post for a target and then fired. Needless to say neither of us got anywhere near what we were aiming at though at the very least we now know which end to hold the gun. David got a little frightened when I explained something to him and gesticulated with the gun in my hand. Thank the Lord, it didn't go off unexpectedly. I'm now ready to take the lead role in 'Annie Get Your Gun.'

Ned Sherlock was not a patient man. He was occasionally a kind and considerate man, but when he could no longer get any sense out of a plaintiff, he'd hand him or her over to the nearest employee of Her Majesty's Colonial Service. On one particular occasion, it happened to be me.

An inconsolable Native woman named Silelele Nkumba stood before me on one of those days when court dockets from the BSA Police were piled high on my desk, when half the messengers were out sick and Anderson was in the bush on some sort of mission he'd conjured up. She spoke little English.

"You have to find the father of this woman," Sherlock demanded. "She hasn't produced a child. Her husband wants a divorce and he cannot get a divorce unless her father gives permission. She hasn't seen the man, who she thinks is her father, for many years. Husband irate, wife ashamed, father missing. Those are the facts.

I'm washing my hands of this one. It's a woman's job."

"I wouldn't know where to begin," I pleaded.

"'It's a wise man who knows his own father. It's a wise woman who knows the father of her child.'" Sherlock, the king of quotations, showed no mercy.

"So, how am I going to find him?" I asked.

"The mother must have an inkling — any one of the men she cohabited with will do. And, by the way, she doesn't know how old she is."

"The mother or the daughter?"

"Both of them probably, it's a mathematical challenge," and with that he left for the Mine Club to have lunch, followed by a couple of gin and tonics to wash it down.

Meanwhile, poor Silelele, every morning she'd walk up the kopje, every morning she'd wait for her mother, and every day her miserable husband would sit as far away as he could from her, hoping this would be the day he'd gain his freedom.

Finally, the mother arrived with a gaggle of older women, all jabbering at the same time and giving perishing looks at the husband, who was now totally outnumbered. They demanded return of the lobola.

He said he wasn't giving it back.

They said no lobola, no divorce.

He said he would return two goats and three chickens. Not the cow. The cow gave milk, the wife gave nothing.

After three days of argument, an mdala — an old man — said he thought he might be Silelele's father, and the divorce was granted.

The women grabbed hold of the two goats that were munching their way through my wastepaper basket, cornered three chickens that had pecked their way through the screening on my window, and left with Silelele.

The next day the-ex husband of Silelele came to my office with another woman, carrying a young child, and asked Sherlock to marry them.

CHAPTER 13

Creatures Great and Small

A game reserve surrounded Wankie, and therein lived all species of indigenous creatures. There were times animals wandered into the town and landed up outside Calamas's store, delving into dustbins, breaking down fences, causing havoc. We had reports of an elephant with her baby stripping leaves off newly planted trees, a giraffe, more legs than body towering over the small shack at the back of the store, and the ever present baboons jumping and landing wherever they pleased — if quick enough, managing to stay alive with tails intact. And close to our rondavels we had bats at night, colorful hunting spiders during the day, and snakes of all varieties. Those I feared the most.

A European came into my office holding a snake in one hand and a handkerchief wrapped around his other hand. The snake was dead.

"Do you know what sort of snake this is?" he asked.

I ran into Sherlock's office, both to avoid the snake and to seek help. "You have a book on snakes?" I demanded.

"Haven't you got anything better to do than study herpetology at the government's expense?"

"I hate snakes, and there's man in my office holding one and he wants to know what kind it is."

He handed me a manual with as much concern as if I'd asked him for a glass of water. "Look it up."

Back in the office the snake had been removed by one of the messengers. The bandaged bloke wasn't looking too healthy. "Got any brandy?"

"This is an office of Her Majesty's government, not a bar," Anderson announced.

"Why do you want to know what sort of snake it is?" I asked, paging through the manual.

"Because it bit me, and I don't feel too well."

Anderson ran out, demanding to see the snake. He came back in a flash. "You don't need a bloody book — that's a black mamba — it's lethal." He took a knife from his belt, pulled the handkerchief off the hunter's arm, sliced the wound, made a tourniquet and shouted for a driver. "Get him out of here before he drops dead on the floor!"

By the time the messengers carried him into the Land Rover, the hunter had lost consciousness. Anderson drove him to the hospital.

Sherlock watched them drive off. "These hunters get mauled, bitten and trampled on, and still they hunt. There's a government pamphlet somewhere in this office, warning them of the hazards of hunting. You're supposed to hand it out when they apply for a licence."

"I know, and I do. You think they bother to read it? They just want to get out in the bush and shoot something. And, by the way, I've never had to issue a hunting license to a woman." The implication hadn't gone unheard.

"Just because women don't hunt . . . "

'nuff said.

David came to pick me up at lunchtime. We had a reservation at the Mine Club restaurant, where one could have a decent enough meal at a reasonable price — better than anything George served up.

David studied the menu.

"Did you see the hunter with the snake bite?" I asked. For some reason, I couldn't get the man and the snake out of my mind.

"Dead on arrival — the snakes around here are poisonous, he should have known."

"Yes, but still . . . "

"If I sympathized with everything l witness at the hospital, I'd be an emotional wreck. He came to us too late." David went back to studying the menu. "Now what you having? I fancy the shepherd's pie."

Later, back at the office, I found the hunter's backpack, and in it a letter from his wife or maybe a girlfriend, a photo of a young child, his address in England and his passport. I had the necessary information to fill in the death certificate:

Name: Nigel Henderson, aged 27, born in Glastonbury,
    Somerset, England
Died: Wankie, Southern Rhodesia, November 4th 1954
Occupation: Hunter
Cause of death: cardiac arrest due to snake bite
Place of burial: yet to be determined

Neville Sherlock sat at his desk composing a condolence letter to the hunter's family. "Not easy to do," he said as he sat back in his chair.

I gave him the death certificate to sign.

"Knowing nothing about the man, I can't be too effusive. It's not the first time this has happened, and it won't be the last. These chaps just turn up, full of self importance, and think they can take on Africa. Africa has its own way of teaching a lesson." He picked up his pen, "I can't write what I should write."

"What's that?

"They should go on safari to see wildlife, not come here to slaughter them."

Was Nigel Henderson a runaway, trying to find himself on the Dark Continent? Was he a dedicated destroyer of wildlife or just a young adventurer proving his manhood in unfriendly terrain? We'll never know. The cemetery in Bulawayo is full of men like him. Cecil Rhodes, himself — buried close by in the Matopos on what he called The Top of the World — was drawn to Africa, like Livingstone and Stanley before him, willing to suffer disease and court death, seeking to inherit the fruits of their explorations.

Sherlock took out his tobacco pouch, filled his pipe and lit it. "That young man was out of his depth, in the wrong place at the wrong time."

It gave me pause to think of my own situation. "I never thought I'd land up here, in the bush. As for this office . . . "

Sherlock interrupted, saying, "I have to be honest, even for me Wankie's a challenge. There's a reason it's considered a hardship posting: more rural, miles from anywhere, and hotter than hell. Still, it is what it is. I'll settle — always do — it's the nature of the job, far superior to a nine-to-five dull existence."

"Then you know how I felt when we first arrived."

"Absolutely. Looks to me you've adapted better than most. Few would have done as well." He signed the certificate. "By the way, I'd like to take you and the good doctor to the Matopos. There's something about it you won't find anywhere else." He studied the calendar on the wall. "How about next weekend? I have a friend in Bulawayo, the Matopos are close by, we can stay with him."

David accepted the invitation, only too pleased to get away from the hospital for a while.

Mother Superior grudgingly gave him the weekend off.

The journey to the Matopos was much the same as the first one we took to Wankie with Delaney. Sherlock, like Delaney, drove like a lunatic, with one difference: Sherlock knew every bump, every twist, and every rock. He found side tracks through the bush, cursing when he came across oversized ant hills and elephant dung. He slowed down to allow a herd of zebra through and gave way to rhinos as they lumbered from one side of the strips to the other. We stopped when we reached Dett, the Rhodesia Railways headquarters in his Matabele district.

"Got to make a courtesy call. You get what you want at the concession store. I won't be long," Sherlock said.

The store sold everything from farm equipment to warm beer. David purchased a packet of Rothman cigarettes, I settled on a bottle of Fanta and a Cadbury bar.

A bus load of Natives had just drawn in and parked next to us. Off they jumped, carrying chickens in cages and babies on their backs. Those traveling on the roof of the bus climbed off, those unwilling to wait threw packages out of windows and quickly followed the same way, others emerged with their belongings from the one narrow door. This was obviously the end of their journey.

"He should turn off the engine," I said, back in the car and closing the windows against the black smoke erupting from the exhaust pipe of the bus.

"Won't do that!" David shouted against the noise of the engine and the loud chatter from its passengers. "He's afraid it won't start up again!"

Men, women and children walked away in the direction of their various villages. This was as far as the bus could take them. They had come from Bulawayo. The moment the last one got off, those waiting for the bus scrambled to get on board, hoping for a seat; if not, onto the roof they climbed.

It was hot and dusty, and we were more than ready to travel on when Sherlock came back carrying a bag of biltong and a flagon of water.

"Great stuff, biltong. A few sticks of this and enough water can keep you going for days in the bush. The Afrikaners introduced biltong to us. They take strips of beef, kudu or ostrich, salt them, dip them in vinegar, add coriander and pepper then hang them out to dry. Doesn't matter that flies cling to it or birds sweep down on it — by the time they take it down it's hard and tasty and ready to eat. You ready? Got to beat the bus, don't want to be stuck behind it all the way to Bulawayo."

There was nothing other than the occasional kraal between Dett and Bulawayo, just a long, winding strip road meandering precariously through bush country. About halfway, David took over the driving while sharp-eyed Sherlock directed us away from hazardous pot holes and fallen branches. A pebble hit the windscreen and a slow crack began to travel down the glass.

"Look, it's creeping all the way down from the impact." David pulled over.

Sherlock, not in the least perturbed, instructed David to carry on. "If we stop for every bit of crud that jumps up on us, we'll never get anywhere. I defy you to find a windscreen in Matabeleland that doesn't have a crack in it. No sense replacing them, it will only happen again — small price to pay for having wheels and not having to walk."

Five hours after leaving Wankie we arrived in Bulawayo, with its streets wide enough to turn around an ox cart, its co-lonial architecture, and its lovely parks — a legacy of Rhodes.

"Bulawayo means 'the place of killing,' " Sherlock told us. "It was here in the Zulu wars that Chaka Zulu made his stand and where I began my colonial service, same age as you, greener than any greenhorn sent out to Africa. Started as a clerk and worked my way up. Not set foot in England since."

"You don't miss it, then?"

"No — this is my home now. Did my bit in the war helping the young pilots who came to train here. Would love to have been one myself but didn't have the eyesight for it. So, here I am and here I stay. Now, you have a choice, you can go posh at the Cecil Hotel or stay a bit rough with me and my friend."

"I think The Cecil Hotel, if you don't mind." I couldn't wait to get into a real bathtub with water I knew would run hot and not suddenly spurt out cold. "I hope you don't mind."

"Not at all, I'll be 'round in the morning, say ten, to set off for the Matopos. That's if I'm not plied with too much booze. I'll do my best to stay sober. Whisky, the curse of the colonials: can't live without it, probably won't live too long with it. By the way, have you noticed what's written on the back of the pound note? Take a look — it's around the edge, it's from a poem by Kipling — read at Rhode's funeral. Says, '. . . *the immense and brooding spirit still shall quicken and control, living, he was the land, and dead, his soul shall be her soul.*' We're not more than ten miles from where Rhodes' heart is buried. The rest of him lies under the floor of Westminster Abbey."

Although saying very little about our excursion, the follow-ing morning Sherlock drove us through an expanse of open bush and scrub-covered hills until we caught sight of a most astonishing phenomenon: huge rocks balanced one upon another in a magical landscape. It was as if we had travelled back into the Stone Age.

Balancing rocks in the Matopos

It's a long climb up to where Cecil Rhodes is said to be interred and to stand beside his grave and the graves of the men who requested to be buried near him. The wind blows, causing eerie musical notes, as it rushes through the immense rocks on which colored lichens, suggested tints and vibrant colors all glow in the warmth of the sun. The grandeur of the scenery and the presence of the graves demand silence, command respect. Respect not only for the dead inscribed but for those who do not have a memorial in their name, those who perished defending their spiritual home against warriors and white men encroaching, wanting to steal their land.

Thoughts, not words, for words can only disturb the solemn panorama that greets you as you stand upon the well worn granite, almost shiny from the footsteps of the curious who, over the years, have come to pay homage and to experience what it is that drew so many to the natural phenomenon of the Matopos. But that is not all there is in the Matopos.

There are caves and more balancing rocks, and on each rock sits a family of baboons. You walk in silence, you gaze in wonderment, for here in the shadow of brave men who came

"HERE LIE THE REMAINS OF CECIL JOHN RHODES"

to this place, battles were fought, agreements were signed and tribes scattered. This is the place where spirits guide the Ngangas, Sangomas and Mhondoros. This is the place where witch doctors pray for rain, for health and for bountiful crops. In these caves there are prehistoric paintings of animals and spear-throwing figures and other imagined scenes, hard to interpret. In these caves sacrifices are still made to the gods, and hermits hide out. Outside, giraffe, buffalo, wildebeests, zebra, warthog and beautiful birds roam among the balancing rocks.

We are in the Rhodes Matopos National Park, a place of beauty and sadness. Sadness for the indigenous African, whose ancestors had lived here for close on forty thousand years, later forced to move, to abandon their guiding spirits and instead pay homage to the white man, who could not hear the voices or communicate with the spirits. Yet the white man could not ignore the fact that the Matopos had something compelling about it, something that kept calling them back, unseen, unidentified, dwelling amongst the balancing rocks of this ancient sight. Why else would Rhodes, an Englishman living in Cape Town, South Africa ask to be buried here?

I sat and pondered the scene — and emotionally moved by it all, I wrote in my notebook:

There is a place where massive granite rocks balance precariously, one on top of the other, forming sculptures of infinite beauty. There is a place where the air is still and where wild life roam, the rhinoceros and the scurrying warthog, the kudu and the ever present scheming baboon. A place where nothing over centuries of time has changed, where a troubled soul can find tranquility and where the spirits of generations long gone are summoned to advise, to give comfort. That place is the Matopos.

I think, when I die, this where I want to be buried.

30th November 1954

. . . David and I are in Bulawayo. It is a very pretty town where every street is lined with Jacaranda trees, where perfume from the flowers of this tree permeate their surroundings. We saw where they held the Rhodes Centenary in 1953 which the Queen Mother and Princess Margaret attended and all in

all I got a far better impression of Bulawayo than I did of Johannesburg. The Matopos had to have had the same impact on Rhodes for he wrote:

'I admire the grandeur and loneliness of the Matopos in Rhodesia, and therefore I desire to be buried in the Matopos on the hill which I used to visit and which I called the View of the World in a square to be cut in the rock on the top of the hill, covered in a plain brass plate with these words thereon.'

And his wishes were carried out. Except David explained it was thought that only his heart was in buried in the grave.

Like so many before me, I gazed in wonderment, reading the inscription on Starr Jameson's grave, looking over miles of bush land below. David, at Wilson's grave, Sherlock beside the memorial to the men of the Shagani patrol who were slaughtered by Chief Lobengula's men. Each of us alone with our thoughts; this was not a place for conversation.

The Lizard Man

The lizard man sat, crossed-legged, beside a granite boulder, a bag of bread crumbs next to him, calling the lizards to him: blue and red, green and orange colored lizards, all controlled by this Ndbele tribesman. He beckoned stop, and they stopped. He beckoned come, and they raced to him, circled him, and left when he ordered them to leave. A simple man with mesmerizing control over these obedient lizards, there had to be a reason for his ability to tame them in so simple a way. Was he, himself, a spirit dressed in government khaki who'd ventured out of a cave in human form? He spoke to no one. There was no one to ask. He was known as "the lizard man," and, for a few pennies thrown into his hat on the ground, he would perform his magic.

Chiefs and headmen from many different areas came to consult the spirits, to stay a while, to wonder at the rocks, to feel their energy like an electric current linked to a wired pole, only there was no pole, no obvious outlet, it just emanated from the structures of rocks, balanced one on top of another, granite monsters, immovable, unyielding, shaped by nature and named by man. "Mother and Child," "Lovers," "Old Man Stooping," "A Pouncing Leopard" — European titles replaced African names. View them from one angle, they are as they were called, see them from another, name them what you will. God, the sculptor, to whom we attribute that which we cannot fathom for ourselves, had no need for a chisel or a hammer, only the elements to chip and wear away the granite. With the rain and the wind and essence of time, He created unforgettable sculptures, individual pieces in an open wall-less gallery, indestructible monoliths there from the beginning of time to remain exactly where they stand long after we are gone.

From The View of the World we descended to the flat lands. Sherlock took us to watch the sable kudu graze, to a kraal where African wardens lived with their families, and to a sacred cave few people knew, let alone would be able to find — a massive opening, going deep within — and there before us a natural theatre with an open arena.

"We can only surmise what went on here," Sherlock said. "We know it was used at one time as a shrine. It held so many clues. A hallowed place to make offerings to the gods and to the spirits, to ask for favors and to sacrifice animals, to plead to be relieved of spells cast upon them by Sangomas or angry relatives. And many would stay for months listening to the spirits. They'd talk to snakes, live safely beside leopards and commune with monkeys. And later they returned to their kraals, older, wiser men, respected and revered, for they had travelled far and stayed long in the cave and learned the secrets of their ancestors."

On the drive back to Wankie Sherlock spoke about his early days in Rhodesia when he travelled on horseback to get to the outlying areas. Often he was greeted by spear carrying Natives who'd guide him to kraals where he'd meet with chiefs and headmen, trying to understand their needs, helping to negotiate tribal differences. He watched the Europeans flood in after the Second World War, changing the characteristics of the country. They formed a thriving metropolis in the two main cities, Salisbury in Mashonaland and Bulawayo in Matabeleland, the latter keeping its small town flavour.

The Shona people of Mashonaland, a less warring tribe, still held grievances against the Ndebeles, a branch of the Zulu tribe. Mistakes were made by government and missionaries. Too late to make amends. The future was uncertain.

Some say Rhodes was a tyrant, others called him a man of vision. I sense he was a bit of both. He opened up the land, he created industry, he brought the modern world to a primitive people, and he allowed missionaries to spread the word of Christ while belittling the gods they'd long worshipped.

Did they want us here? Some did, others resented us and still do.

One day, I believe, we will pay a huge price for our empirical conquest, and it won't be only us who suffer, it will be the people we will be forced to leave behind, those caught between what we created and the lifestyle they once knew. Fifty or maybe sixty years is not long enough to make a lasting change. For now we must do what we can.

5th December 1954

*The journey back from Bulawayo was awful, rain-
ing hard all the way; it took five and a half hours.
We drove through flooding waters and thick mud,
this time not getting stuck in it — the strips in part
had been completely washed away and we just had
to guess their whereabouts. When I wasn't at the
wheel my job was to look for elephants, and when
David was at the wheel his job was to criticize my
driving. Sherlock said he drove down he wasn't
driving back so he slept most of the way. A baboon
jumped from a tree right in front of the car but we
managed to avoid it, David was ready with gun in
hand. "Put it away," I said, "you'll probably miss
and then we'll have a bullet hole in the car and a
baboon laughing at us from his perch high up in a
tree. We didn't need the five shillings we could have
collected for the deed. I'm far happier being five
shillings poorer . . . had a letter from Renee who
tells me you are frightened out of your life about
us having a gun . . . with what I just wrote you will
probably worry more — now don't be a silly old
thing — we keep it in the car and probably won't
touch it again until we leave. It's far safer to have
one at hand in case of an emergency so don't think
another thing about it. As for scorpions and creepy
crawlies I have now resigned myself to the fact that
I will have to live with them for the next fifteen
months so I might as well put up with them. I'm not
nearly as squeamish as I was, in fact the lizards and
I have come to an agreement — they eat the insects
and I let them share our accommodations.*

Chapter 14

A Romanian in Africa

After the rains came cooler weather. More at ease now with my surroundings, I decided to walk to the office each morning. Delaney added house calls to David's already overworked schedule, so his car wasn't available and mine refused to go up the hill. The NC's vehicles were often out on government business.

This particular morning I was walking toward the turnoff to the kopje when a car pulled up behind me.

"You a Jew?" the driver shouted.

Without hesitating and gearing up for a fight, I answered defiantly, "Yes, I am."

He slowed down and stuck his head out the window, "I'm the other one. I heard a rumor. My wife, me, we Jews. Come to dinner Friday night! We have concession store in Madumabisa — take Falls Road, turn at sign on dirt path. We live in house behind the store."

He drove off as if it were the most normal thing to do to ask someone, to whom he hadn't been introduced to or even set eyes on before, to come for Sabbath dinner. I didn't know his name, he didn't know mine. When I reached the office I asked if anyone knew the owner of the concession store in Madumabisa. They all knew him.

"He's a Romanian immigrant, a gymnast," Anderson replied. "Don't be surprised if he greets you hanging upside down from a bar or a branch of a tree. I'm told he's a holocaust survivor. Interesting chap, a bit peculiar, his wife runs the store while he practices for the next Olympic games."

No one knew his telephone number and, anyway, he probably didn't have one. I could perhaps send a runner, but it was a bit too far, and Sherlock, always the optimist when it came to food, assured me Romanian cuisine wasn't nearly as bad as Afro-European cooking, so why not give it a go? "And, if you're driving at night, take a torch, a gun and a can of petrol."

Sherlock held up the rifle he kept in his office and handed it to me. "Take this with you."

"A gun? What am I supposed to do with this? I hope you're not suggesting I have to hunt for my dinner in Madumabisa?"

"Keep it in the car."

"But we have a gun in the car."

"You have a pistol. This is a proper gun."

He called for Ndozwi to set up a target at the back of the office. "I'm told you've had one practice attempt. You'll need more."

I followed Ndozwi to a sandy patch where he'd set up a target. The first shot I fired nearly knocked me over as the gun kicked back in my shoulder. I have no idea where the bullet went.

Ndozwi came over to show me how to hold the rifle, "Strong, Medem, strong." I gripped it as I was shown, took aim and fired.

Half a dozen Natives came out of the bushes, yelling and screaming, running for their lives.

"Sorry, I didn't know you were there!" I shouted. I could have been charged with murder. The third shot ricocheted off a rock and barely missed Sherlock's dog.

Sherlock stood at the back window watching. "Useless, absolutely useless. Give me the gun back. You'll be safer without it."

"One more try, please."

The third shot actually clipped the side of the bull's-eye. "See, I'm improving," I called back.

"All right, take it and pray you won't have to use it. Remember, you're going off the beaten track and that means animals large and small. Lion, elephant, you name it, could be roaming, and I don't want you coming face to face with any of them — don't shoot at them, shoot in the air and, hopefully, whatever it is will scurry off."

I refrained from writing to my parents about my target practice, having told them I'd probably never have the need to use a weapon. But then I decided to own up and send them the photo Sherlock took. I wondered if they noticed I was holding the gun the wrong way 'round.

12th December 1954

. . . yesterday I had a shooting lesson outside my office. One of the messengers fixed up a bulls eye for a target — actually two circles drawn on a piece of board. David said I should stick to being Clerk of the Court, issuing gun licences, not firing them. He thinks that's the closest I should ever get to any weapon. And looking at the enclosed photo you will most likely agree with him. The magistrate has had to go to take court at the Victoria Falls and crime here seems to have settled down a bit. I've had the odd native divorce to deal with. One woman came up this morning, got her divorce, went home and then came back to say she had changed her mind — she loves her old man after all and can the divorce be cancelled — always willing to oblige I tore up the form and now everyone is happy again — imagine that happening in England. I expect her back in a few

days to say she's changed her mind again. It really doesn't matter because the men have many wives and probably won't take much notice of her anyway. Look at the enclosed photograph. Only tried a pistol so far — not nearly as difficult as the weapon you can see they've handed me for our next practice outing.

David was prepared to go anywhere for a decent meal, even to a bloke he'd never set eyes on. George, our cook, had not improved his culinary skills. He managed breakfast, but when instructed to make sandwiches for lunch he'd cut the bread in "doorstep slices," plonk on leftovers from last night's supper and proudly serve them as if he'd created a Cordon Bleu masterpiece. And his enthusiasm for cabbage continued.

Cabbage was served with every meal. Where it came from, I hadn't a clue. Calamas didn't sell it. It wasn't growing anywhere I could see. Yet every day it turned up. I asked George nicely not to serve it, still it arrived every day hidden under meat or chicken, brought in a covered dish and even served cold as an hors d'oeuvre.

Then I found out it wasn't cabbage, it was some green leaf thing they ate in the villages. I tried a new tack. "You have it, George, please. We don't want to take your food."

My attempt to dissuade him had little effect. George's cabbage was ever present, a plant that had no season, a botanical mystery that grew without cultivation, an African staple that had kept them fed for centuries.

"Very good, Medem, make me strong, make you strong — have lots of babies."

I wasn't ready for lots of babies. George could keep his cabbage, and if I insulted him by not eating it, so be it.

The only babies I had anything to do with since my arrival in Wankie were ones I could admire and give back. So many of the Native mothers I'd met had little ones hanging on their skirts or strapped to their back: babies I held while their mothers came to look for jobs, babies I held when sending their mother's to Ngomahuru, babies I held when the father came in to say it wasn't his and I should do something about it.

✉

14th December 1954

. . . your first grand-child? Unfortunate-ly I had to give him back and you'll have to wait till we can make one of our own . . . we are buying tickets for the Rhodesian sweep stake, one for you, too, first prize ten thousand pounds. If you receive a rather large cheque you'll know where it

Sampling motherhood

comes from. Don't spend it all at once — oh and let me know your nom de plume — can't put your actual name on it, don't want the world clamoring at your door for donations.

It was growing dark when we left for Madumabisa. Bats flying, kudu caught in the headlights, while Natives walked on the edge of the dirt road. Unless they were wearing something white it was hard to distinguish them from the trees. David lowered his speed. He wasn't taking any chances, should someone or some creature wander across his path: he would be able to brake in time. He tried to avoid pot holes and rocks, but having missed one there was always another.

I thought I saw a lion, could be a leopard, prowling the bush, ready to pounce. Danger seemed to lurk behind every tree. We had the loaded rifle at the back of the car. Having it available made me feel a little safer, even though I was scared to touch it, let alone use it. David wasn't any good with it either.

Together with the gun, Sherlock insisted I take a couple of flares and a box of matches, explaining if we got into trouble we'd light them and hope someone would come to our rescue. "Don't set the bush on fire," Sherlock warned, "make sure the match is out before you chuck it away."

Night birds screamed, crickets chirped, fireflies hovered. I was breathing so hard my breath began to steam up the windows.

David concentrated on the road, his bright lights on, his hands tightly clasped on the wheel. He was a city boy; he could drive in traffic, but not so confident on a moonlit night, traveling a dirt road that stretched out before him with apparently no end. He didn't relish the return journey, and then, quite without warning, a warthog stood in front of us, his eyes unblinking in the headlights.

David stopped the car. An ugly, snorting creature. Nothing we could do but wait and hope he would move on. David switched off the ignition and turned off the headlights. We watched it scamper away into the dark. Only the sounds of animals foraging remained.

We waited, not saying a word. Immediate danger had passed. David turned on the engine and we continued our journey to Madumabisa until, out of nowhere, a bright light shone in the distance. I thought we might be there, though without

Warthog

any identification it was hard to tell. I saw a petrol pump and behind it a store that seemed to be closed. No sign of life.

"Whatever-his-name told me they live behind the store, so the house has to be close by." I presumed.

"That's all you know? He didn't tell you where he actually lived?"

"He did — behind the store."

"I don't know why I put you in charge of directions."

"I spent no more than two minutes with the man. It's not exactly crowded out here — if there's something that looks like a house, it's his."

We left the car outside the store and walked to the back. A Native came toward us. He said he worked for the owners and indicated we should follow him. No, he didn't know their name, just called them Nkos and Nkosikas (Mr. and Mrs.). They'd told him to wait for us by the petrol pump in front of the store.

In fact, the house was not just behind the store, it was at least a fifteen minute walk from where we parked the car. Had I known the distance between the store and their house, I'd have opted for boots. I hadn't yet got it into my head that the bush was no place for high heels!

On arrival we were greeted by the man who'd invited us. He was jumping on a homemade trampoline. At the sight of us he performed one last acrobatic maneuver, landing right in front of where we stood. He looked every bit the athlete.

"I am Marcus," he announced, "and my wife, she is Bianca. Welcome. Bianca has made dinner. She will not have a cook." He hardly took a breath. "We had one when we first came here. She tried to teach him Romanian recipes, but he did not understand our ways. We have him working in the store. Come, we welcome you to our home."

Bianca, middle aged, short and plump, came out of the kitchen as we were ushered in. Her English was halting, little wonder she confused the cook. She kissed me on both cheeks, didn't know quite what to do with David, so he eased the situation and gave her a hug.

She beckoned us to a table covered with a white cloth. Two

candlesticks stood beside a loaf of bread. She lit the candles then poured two glasses of sweet wine. Marcus placed a yarmulke on his head, gave one to David and recited the Sabbath prayers.

Bianca said something in Romanian. Marcus translated: "She says you are the first Jews she has met in Africa and she is very happy you are here."

"And we are happy you invited us," I said.

"Sit, sit. Bianca will bring the food. You drink? I have schnapps, whisky, vodka, anything you like," Marcus offered excitedly.

"I'll have a whisky, thank you," David replied.

"Only if you let me drive home," I stage whispered. It was hard enough getting there sober, Lord knows what it might be like after he had a few drinks.

"Then make it a small one. I'm not having my wife in the driving seat in the pitch dark."

"And you?" Marcus asked me.

"Just a cold drink, it seems I'm the navigator." I gave my husband a look to let him know I did not appreciate his comments about my driving skills.

Bianca came in with a tureen full of something I did not recognize.

"Aah, my favorite dish — brains." Marcus was in heaven.

Even George's cabbage sounded more inviting than brains. I couldn't be rude and refuse, but they looked awful — globby white things with vegetables in thick, white gravy.

"Eat, Eat. We have plenty." Marcus tucked a bib into his shirt and ladled Bianca's concoction onto his plate.

I'd gone through a similar experience when I first arrived in Johannesburg. David's aunt served calf's foot jelly as a hors d'oeuvre and tripe for the main meal. Hadn't they heard of matzo balls and chicken soup? Did they all have to eat the innards and the feet of the animals they slaughtered? I had to think of a way out of my predicament.

"I am sorry, Bianca, I'm a vegetarian," I lied. "I'll just eat the vegetables."

Bianca appeared crestfallen.

David looked askance.

Bianca went into a long harangue in Romanian with Marcus, which I imagine had something to do with whether she should offer me another dish.

"We have fruit and cake — you like fruit and cake?"

"I love fruit and cake."

She started for the kitchen.

"Please, Bianca, sit down and have your dinner," I urged.

I separated the glob from the veggies — not an easy task. White potatoes, white turnips, white onions — not a trace of color anywhere.

David saved the evening by asking how they landed up in Madumabisa, an African village not even on the map. Bianca looked on, living it again, while Marcus related their story. It held me enthralled.

"I stay alive in Belsen, Bianca in Auschwitz. We met after the war in DP, displacement camp in Judenburg. We fell in love — I did not want to stay in Europe — too many memories."

Bianca spoke.

Marcus interpreted. "She wants you to know we, she as well as me, had to get away from Europe."

I reached out to touch Bianca's hand.

"I trained as gymnast, my parents insist I study engineering. We all displaced persons need to start new life. I find a job on ship leaving for South Africa. Bianca, she work in kitchen. On the ship we hear about Rhodesia and decided to go there.

"The ship docked in Cape Town, we got off. I spoke a little English. I had a little money. I joined a circus. The circus came to Rhodesia. Bianca made my costumes. Then I met a man, he worked in Wankie. He said he was driving there, we could drive with him. And — well, too much story — here we are in Madumabisa. I bought bricks and wood, and build this house"

He thought a moment and added, "We have no family. Our parents, our sisters, our brothers, died, murdered in concentration camps. We have each other. It is enough."

Bianca and Marcus were the first holocaust victims I'd met. My war, the same war, was bombs falling out of the sky. Theirs was atrocities. I had been saved from what they were forced to experience. I felt dreadful, spoiled and shamed. I couldn't eat their food, I'd complained all the way to where they lived, and here I was seated with two remarkable people who'd made a life for themselves in a foreign land, after having witnessed firsthand the Nazi tyranny.

That evening, that encounter, would have a lasting effect.

I spoke little on our way back to Wankie, except to say, "I will never complain about anything ever again."

CHAPTER 15

Christmas, Food and Sex

✉

26th December 1954 — Boxing Day

David was on duty so after a late breakfast we made our way to the hospital. Nothing was doing in the European section so we went down to the African section. There great festivities were going on — choirs singing, drums playing and all the patients out of their beds drinking kaffir beer, a foul concoction of fermented mealie meal and odd vegetables made into a disgusting drink. The nurses were trying their best to make the place as bright and gay as possible, but if you could only see the squalor and hardship of this pitiful place you would understand that their job was not an easy one. I was handed a few toys, comics and clothes and followed the nurses around distributing. This was Christmas in Wankie, a festival for the natives alone. They get paralytic drunk, they turn up for work when they feel like it, and they fight like cats and dogs. Very few know the real meaning of the day, but that doesn't seem to matter because it is the one day in the year they can let themselves go and still be within the arm of the law. We went down to the compound to watch their games and tribal dances. This spectacle is really something to see and the incessant beat of the drums reminds one only too well of the primitive instincts of these people. David took a lot of photographs and we will send them to you — you won't of course capture the colour and gaiety, but you will be able to see and feel the air of complete abandonment that comes on such a festive and to them unique occasion. David spent most of the evening stitching up Africans.

I received my Jewish Cook Book — I think I'll ask Bianca and Marcus for dinner, I can't get them out of my mind, two remarkable people who survived the holocaust — they served brains — I'll serve chicken. Did you ever buy brains, Mummy? I know the answer — what it always was, don't ask what it is, just eat it, there's a war on! Today we have been married six months; we have done so much in that time and visited so many places in fact it all seems like a wonderful dream and every now and then I pinch myself to see whether I really am awake and sober.

Only it wasn't a dream — it was only too real.

The indictments continued to pour into the Native Commissioners Office and Sherlock jokingly blamed the heavy load on me. "It's those young police fellows — any excuse to come up here and chat with you."

"I'm a married woman," I reminded him. Actually, I enjoyed the repartee with the young constables, who were closer to me in age than any of the chaps working in the office and even younger than my husband, who was seven years older than me.

"Makes no difference, married or not, a cat can look at a king," Sherlock quipped and then quoted from the anonymous poem it came from:

Some hear and see him whom he heareth nor seeth not
But fields have eyes and woods have ears, ye wot
And also on my maids he is ever tooting.
Can ye judge a man, (quoth I), by his looking?
What, a cat may look on a king, ye know!

29th December 1954

Everyone in the office has a hangover except me —
Sherlock had a cocktail party last night. His poor
servants got more than they bargained for and are
keeping out of sight. Successful parties rely on one
ingredient, booze. As long as there is plenty of whisky,
gin, brandy and port everyone has a good time. Li-
quor is cheap: whisky twenty two shillings a bottle,
Gin, ten and sixpence . . . my fizzy lemonade about
four pence. I'm not breaking the bank with that.

The British South Africa Police were responsible for maintain-
ing law and order in the vast territories between the Limpopo
and Zambezi Rivers and the Bechuanaland Protectorate on the
West and Portuguese East Africa on the East. These territories
became Southern Rhodesia and Northern Rhodesia, named
after Cecil Rhodes. They were the fellows who kept order in
Wankie and brought charges against the law breakers. And one
of those culprits was Sixpence Nkoto.

Sixpence Nkoto was accused of rape and scheduled to
appear in Native Court. The day before the hearing I was
told the case had been dismissed. I'd prepared for the case,
scheduled it, and now it had been called off.

I was baffled and cornered Monty when he came up to retrieve the paperwork. "So, what's all this about, not to mention
the woman he attacked, either he raped her or he didn't." I was
becoming quite brazen.

Monty agreed with me. He'd spent half his day getting all the evidence, interviewing the defendant, speaking to the village Chief, getting all the necessary information, and then the woman Sixpence supposedly raped came forward to admit he didn't rape her. He was her boyfriend. Her father made her bring charges.

"Why?"

"Because they performed the act on the public footpath leading to the father's kraal and the villagers complained,"

"Then it wasn't rape?"

"No, it had to do with where the act took place."

"I don't get it."

"Neither did I 'til she told me. She'd asked Sixpence if they could go to his hut. They were on their way when he remembered his wife was in his hut and he couldn't bring another woman there . . . I'm not quite sure how to say this . . . "

"Just say it."

"Their desire got the better of them — no, let me get this right — she said his desire got the better of him and he did what he did in a clearing in the bush near a well-used footpath."

"I don't blame her, I'd object, too. Then what happened?"

"People saw them."

29th December 1954

I'm very busy at the Court now typing out annual reports and of course noting the inevitable juicy rape, murder and housebreaking cases. In the three months I have been here we have had more High Court cases than the rest of the year put together. Ned Sherlock, the Magistrate, insists it is because of his voluptuous blond secretary, as he often refers to me — and just between you and me, I too am beginning to wonder. Last night we went to a party at the Police camp — they're all English and

very good fun. We managed to dance a few times,
but the heat was so overpowering that after even a
minor session the perspiration began to pour, and
so we sat back and watched the youngsters enjoy-
ing themselves . . . (Listen to me? I was probably
the youngest there anyway.)

Two days later Sixpence's wife came to my office and asked for a divorce — he had done it again. Must have been something about that footpath that turned him on, I thought. Anyway, that meant Sixpence had to return her lobola, which he couldn't do as they had eaten most of the chickens and traded the goats, and, added to that, they had a child. This was more than I could deal with.

Anderson thought it funny.

Sherlock told them to work it out among themselves.

Monty threw his arms up in the air, jumped on his motorcycle and left for a holiday with his girlfriend at the Victoria Falls Hotel.

This case went on for days. The problem with Native divorces is that entire kraals get involved and they all have an opinion. Finally, I got them to agree to replace the chickens.

Sixpence showed little interest in the child, probably wasn't his, he claimed. "She have many boyfriends — me not only one. Child not look like me. I don't want child."

The father finally accepted the child on condition the goat be returned. I couldn't tell one goat from another. The father said it wasn't the right goat. Ndozwi came to my rescue and threw them all out of my office.

It took about a year before I could no longer be shocked by what came through the Native Commissioners Office. The young officers gave up their practical jokes with various insects and even large animals. Ned Sherlock was my friend as well as my boss. Anderson spent more time out of the office, confident I could do his work as well as mine. The messengers, who were at first wary of a woman in a European man's job, couldn't do enough for me, and it wasn't unusual for the Natives to ask to see me directly when they needed help.

I began to feel at home in an outpost of the British Empire.

26th January 1955

I look forward to the day when we go on a journey without something disastrous happening. We were on our way to a dentist in Bulwayo, I had toothache, and there is no dentist in Wankie. The first obstacle we came across was a fallen tree in the middle of the road but we managed to get around it and that was ok. After that the sun came out and we thought everything was fine but, as we came down to the river, an 'orrible sight awaited us. The water was at least a foot above the bridge and only the top of the railings could be seen. We saw a native walking across and as his hat wasn't floating we decided to take a chance . . . he was lucky, there were plenty of crocodiles gliding around. Our car did very nicely and we reached the other side wet but safe . . . when we came to a straight stretch of the road we saw a native frantically waving, we had no option; we just had to stop. He wanted a lift to Bulawayo. David got out the gun and told him to get in the back. The gun frightened the life out of him and me. He said he worked for a Mrs. Rubinstsein in Bulawayo and was late getting back. As we reached Lupani, a huge Cadillac sidled up to us and the occupant therein informed us that we could go no further; the River Gwaai immediately ahead was rising fast and the other rivers farther along were already badly flooded. That meant if we did get through the first river we wouldn't be able to pass the second and we'd marooned between the two. Luckily there was a hotel nearby and we stopped to talk things over. The native jumped out of the car and fled and we decided to return to Wankie. It was getting dark now and driving on Rhodesia's awful roads at night is no joke and we still didn't know if we'd get through the Gwaai. All the way we had to swerve to avoid various animals that come out at night. Bats were flying, a jackal glared at us, lions roamed, and an enormous snake draped itself across our path — we let him have the right of way. The Gwaai had subsided a little — we covered 216 miles and got nowhere and had to turn back. The moral of the story is never get a toothache in the rainy season in Africa but I have little choice until then I'll be on aspirin til the rivers subside.

CHAPTER 16

What's She Doing in My Hut?

And it was on that trip I came down with malaria, even after taking the anti-malaria pill, Paludrine, once a week, though I'd probably forgotten a couple of times. Obviously, you have to follow the regimen religiously.

Mosquitoes were everywhere: in the puddles, in the thatch above us, hiding in the laundry, even coming out of the taps. When I caught one, it splattered blood, probably mine! The lizards were not doing their job and the chameleons were definitely on strike.

It started with a bad headache. Aspirin didn't touch it. I couldn't hold my head up, and I certainly couldn't work.

"You have malaria. I told you to take your pill on the same day once a week. Why don't you listen to me?" David seemed more annoyed than concerned.

"I did."

"You couldn't have done."

"I'm not in the mood to argue." I had a raging fever and couldn't find a comfortable place to put myself. "Get that awful little girl out of here."

"There's no little girl, you're hallucinating."

He called for Elias to bring a basin of cold water.

"She's there — right by the door — she's got long, stringy hair and skinny legs. Tell her to go away."

I remember Elias arriving with a cloth and water, and then I must have passed out.

The apparition kept vigil. Sometimes she danced at the end of my bed. Other times she sat there making faces at me. She would not leave, and no one could see her but me. My fever lasted four long days before it began to subside. Eventually, she left.

"I never want to see her again," I said, sitting up in bed and sipping a cup of chicken soup George had made for me.

"She's probably gone to visit another idiot who forgot to take their malaria pills," David suggested. Still, I could see he was relieved I'd returned to the living.

It was after my bout of malaria I realized a doctor's wife should never expect to be treated in the loving and caring way her husband treats his patients.

I returned to work only to get the equivalent amount of sympathy from my fellow workers that I received from my husband. Sherlock left a bottle of Paludrine on my desk. Anderson rigged up a mosquito net over my typewriter and Monty gave me a fly swat. I pulled down the net — I wasn't about to sit there like Miss Haversham from *Great Expectations* for the remainder of my time at the Native Commissioners Office. I did, however, remember to take the pill every Friday.

2nd February 1955

I have come to the conclusion this office should be turned into a mental home. This morning we have two lunatics here — one screaming and ranting wanting to fight with everyone and using filthy language — pity he ever learned English — and the other one just sitting quietly staring into space. The quiet one is under the impression the Machusas (a local tribe) had killed his wife, his father and his child. The police investigated and found he never had a family. The fighter broke out of his cell last night because he said there was an entire army with him in his cell and they were going to announce a war and he didn't want to take part. I have made out two orders to get them into the mental home in Ingutsheni but until I receive word from Ingutsheni that there is room for them they will remain in my office. What a job this is to be sure. I deal with lepers to send to the Leprosarium, criminals to jail, greet chiefs, deal with imminent tribal disturbances in fact if you can imagine it, I'm supposed to take care of it . . . I never know what's going to happen next. Ahh excuse me for a moment while I collect twenty-five pounds from a European who socked a native (per Sir Godfrey Huggins) who passed the law that no European is allowed to lift a finger to an African no matter what happens — hence the rather large fine. Well done, Sir Godfrey . . . Just received the result of the census taken in Wankie — there are two thousand Europeans widely scattered, half of them children, and, wait for it, twenty five thousand natives registered the rest not counted or taken in to consideration. If the natives decide to have an uprising we'd be totally outnumbered, don't worry, it's all quiet so far.

I returned to work and immediately Anderson pleaded cabin fever due to my absence and had to get out in the bush to regain his sanity. Sherlock left for an ndaba with the Batonka tribesmen, and Monty decided he'd stay another few days at the Victoria Falls.

David, who'd had it up to his back teeth with the nuns, arranged a meeting with the Chief Medical Officer of the Anglo American Corporation to see if he could find a job in a better location than Wankie.

"So, what did he say?" I asked when he came back from the interview.

"Not much. Seems most of the hospitals out of Bulawayo and Salisbury are run by nuns, and he thinks it better for me to finish my contract here, and if I want to start over, I could look for an equally difficult position elsewhere. In other words, forget it."

"Then we stay?"

"Yes. But if those penguins don't carry out my orders, you may find me up before the magistrate for murder."

"They can't be that bad," I said, trying to ease his disappointment.

"Every time the church bell rings they disappear *en masse* to Mass, and I'm left either holding a scalpel or examining a patient. I've told the Mother Superior over and over again that she must arrange for at least one Sister to stay on duty. I may as well talk to a warthog in the game reserve."

"Then Delaney should put his foot down."

"He won't say a word to them — tells me they're Catholics just like him, and he understands their need for prayer."

15th February 1955

I finally got to go to the dentist, this time by myself and by train. I found that I had to share a compartment with two drunken women and three screaming kids so yours truly collared the guard and demanded a coupe. The train arrived in Bulawayo three hours late the railways lines having been washed away some miles down the track due to the ever persistent rain . . . most transport in Southern Africa has come to a standstill. The roads are impassable and the air strips are too sodden for planes to land. The railways aren't equipped to cope with excess baggage. We've had no mail for days. There is an outbreak of malaria which is difficult to control. We were listening to Radio News Reel the other evening and they were describing the

*unnatural weather in this part of the world. Don't
know when you will receive this letter.*

I refrained from telling my parents I'd already had malaria.
Better they not know. That dreadful little girl still visits me in
nightmares.

We colonials live the good life, we believe. We are doing the
right thing by bringing western values to the indigenous people.
The majority of us treat our servants well and certainly we do
what we can to improve the lives of those who have so little.

The government provides medical services. Our teachers
open schools in rural areas. Our Land Development Officers
show the best way to sow and harvest crops. Our Native and
District Commissioners watch over their districts. We try to
understand tribal customs. We watch over hunters, not allowing them to wipe out endangered species. We provide wells.
We brought electricity and telephones to outlying areas. The
government is building roads and improving the railways.
One day we could become a multi-racial society, unlike South
Africa, where the law is apartheid and will remain so unless
some miracle occurs.

Rhodesia is a young country; it's less than sixty years since
Cecil Rhodes first came here when there was nothing other than
bush. He came with mineral rights arranged by treaties and
influence. He used his own wealth, money derived from gold
mining in South Africa, and made promises he had no intention
of carrying out. He formed the British South Africa Company,
and later became prime minister of the Cape Colony. In years to
come his enormous wealth endowed the Rhodes Scholarships:

*My desire being that the students who shall be
elected to the scholarships shall not merely be book-
worms, I direct that in the election of a student to
a Scholarship regard shall be had to (i) his literary
and scholastic attainments (ii) his fondness of and*

success in manly outdoor sports such as cricket football and the like (iii) his qualities of manhood truth courage devotion to duty sympathy for the protection of the weak kindliness unselfishness and fellowship and (iv) his exhibition during school days of moral force of character and of instincts to lead to and to take an interest in his schoolmates for those latter attributes will be likely in afterlife to guide him to esteem the performance of public duties as his highest aim.

CHAPTER 17

The Good and Not So Good Colonials

I recalled Dr. Delaney saying to me when we first met in Bulawayo, "Africa will get in your blood," and he was right. It couldn't be more in my blood than it was working as Clerk of the Court in the Native Commissioners Office. I knew more about tribal customs and tribal people than most Europeans born in Africa. I learned to respect the ways of the Ndebele and realized just because it wasn't my way didn't mean it was the wrong way.

Wrong were greedy Europeans using Natives to help them make unshared fortunes. Wrong was the way they treated the indigenous people. But none of that applied to us working in the Native Commissioners Office.

The others living in Wankie were the mine officials, the mine overseers and, far too often, their wives, putting on airs and graces. And then we received an invitation to the annual Wankie Colliery Mine Manager's Garden Party.

"Do we have to go?" I asked David.

"Yes."

"Do we have to go?" I asked Sherlock.

"Yes."

Do I have to go? I asked myself.

I didn't have the option. The only thing good about it was it gave me a chance to wear one of my trousseau dresses, which had hung in our makeshift wardrobe since we took up residence in Wankie.

A large and gleaming, pristine white tent was set up on the grounds of the residence of the Mine Manager. Had we been invited to Queen Elizabeth's Birthday celebration at Windsor, it couldn't have been grander. Africans roamed the crowds with silver trays of delicate canapés. The bar, draped in the Union Jack, served every alcoholic beverage imaginable in cut glass goblets. Soft music played from somewhere. The men wore suits and ties. The women — dressed in silks and fine cottons, their hair coiffed, their white gloves spotless — clung to their men like a baboon clings to a rock.

Here we were in the middle of the bush in a town with one melting road, within sight of a coal mine, with rhinos occasionally popping out of the game reserve, with the only store unable to receive deliveries of staple foods because we'd been cut off for days by flooded rivers, and somehow none of it had any effect on the Mine Manager's Garden Party.

After the canapés came the dinner: rare roast beef, fresh vegetables, baby potatoes, freshly baked rolls, second helpings piled on plates, followed by chocolate desserts, fruit salad covered in fresh cream and gourmet cheeses. Did anyone give a thought to the Natives in the compound who were digging themselves out of mud and desperate to save their crops? Did anyone care about the underling Europeans not invited, who stayed home getting drunk on their own liquor? Of course not. We, the privileged, were being treated to an abundance of delicacies not available outside the confines of this obscene spectacle.

Sherlock, looking smart in his white trousers and navy blazer, wandered over. "So you decided to join the fray."

"Under your orders," I replied.

"It's called diplomacy: you scratch my back and I'll scratch yours."

"How do they manage this spread? Where does it come from?"

"Everything flown in from South Africa. May as well make the most of it, tomorrow we're back to what's left in the larder, although I hear they've cleared the tracks on the railway. We should be okay in a couple of days."

We did the rounds. I had little to say to the ladies and they not much to say to me. Typical upper crust colonials: cigarette holders in one hand and drinks in the other, "rings on their fingers and bells on their toes." Well, not exactly, I couldn't see their toes encased in nylon stockings and high heeled shoes, the heels digging into the grass like arrows from a bow.

"Can I get you a gin and tonic?" one of them asked.

"No, thank you, just a cold drink. Lemonade, perhaps?"

"Just try a G and T, you could get accustomed to it," Sherlock suggested. He'd come to my rescue while David discussed medical cases with Delaney.

"Maybe I could get used to this," I said as I accepted the G and T and swilled it down.

"Hold on, girl. That's a strong drink, you're supposed to sip it."

"Oh, well, too late now," I had to admit my head was already spinning.

"I'll get you a lemonade. That's more your style, I can see that."

He was right. I had no tolerance for alcohol and knew little about it. The same bottle of sweet red kosher wine remained in my parent's sideboard for as long as I could remember, brought out once a year at Passover for the Seder service. I recalled seeing an occasional bottle of Guinness at my grandmother's house. She drank it "for medicinal purposes," she said. The sundowner custom of the Rhodesians would never entice me. It may have started as a sundowner tradition early on, but as far as the colonials were concerned, the sun never went down.

David mingled with the crowd, chatting up the ladies, shooting the breeze with the blokes, many of them his patients. I was summarily introduced to a group of women who, after the usual hellos and how-are-you were completed, carried on talking about the problems they were having with their servants. Mrs. Whitechurch's cook had been whisked away by Mrs. Sanderson; she'd coveted him for years. Mrs. Lovell's houseboy had stolen a piece of her silver. Mrs. Robinson found her nanny dead drunk in the servant's quarters.

I could have joined in and told them about George and his eternal cabbage offerings but decided against it. I'd grown fond of George, and he hadn't served cabbage for a while.

"Your man can be quite the charmer when he wants to," Sherlock observed.

"David? As long as he remains in his doctor capacity," I remarked. "He's not much good in other social gatherings."

"Seems to be doing pretty well here," he replied, sipping his Pimm's Cup and eyeing David, hob-knobbing. "Mind you, I can understand doctors must get fed up with all the complaints they have to contend with in and out of working hours."

"I'd have thought the same goes for us — I mean, for you," I answered.

"Maybe so, but we don't have to cure them, only listen to them."

"And the rest is up to the with doctors?"

"If it's one of their diseases, yes. One of ours, then off they go to the hospital."

"Can I go home now?"

Sherlock looked at me like a father observes his daughter. "Give it a little longer — can't rush out before the after-dinner drinks are served."

"Oh, God, not more liquor."

"One of the perks for attending the Mine Manager's Party. Not the gut-eating brandy we get at Calamas. Here they serve Courvoisier. Now, that's worth waiting for."

David and Sherlock enjoyed the party. I couldn't wait to go home.

The uninvited creatures that share our home have now been joined by two puppies of non-denominational variety. They are both black and they are both untrained. David decided I would be safer in the house with a canine companion, so he got two in case one wasn't up to the job. I have called them Dingle and Michael after the Foot Brothers.

Michael, because as a member of parliament he'd recently been dispatched from London to Rhodesia to advise us on how to run the country. Dingle because he's his brother, and it's a good name for a dog. I hadn't been here long enough to call myself a Rhodesian, but I'd been here longer than Michael Foot, who came for a few days and gave his unasked-for opinion. I do not believe an Englishman sitting in parliament in Westminster can possibly know, or for that matter understand, what it is like trying to govern a country with as many problems as this one. I'll keep the dogs and their names. Foot must return to his ancestral home in Devonshire and do what Devonshire people do — make clotted cream.

23rd February 1955

David and I are taking up fishing. We're off to the Zambezi where we will meditate with rods in our hands, and maybe our hours of solitude will bring forth edible rewards. I don't know what I shall do if I happen to catch anything, don't fancy releasing it from the hook, but that is a situation I can deal with should it occur. It's a far safer hobby than crocodile and elephant hunting. I've often wondered what would happen if one shot an elephant and missed. As for crocodiles — don't intend to catch one of those.

The African children here do not have enough reading matter and would really appreciate a little parcel of books from you or anyone. See what you can do, please.

Sherlock has informed me that when I refer to Rhodesia I should give its full title — The Federation of Rhodesia and Nyasaland — which includes Northern and Southern Rhodesia. "The British government joined us together thinking it would counter apartheid in South Africa. Can't see that it's done much, but then it's early days. So, it doesn't matter which side of the Zambezi you fish on — we're all one big happy family now. I'm waiting to see how long it lasts!"

CHAPTER 18

Leprosy, Lightning & Libations

✉

25th February 1955

We had a most dreadful storm today the likes of which I have never seen. It was directly overhead and I had visions of the office taking flight. Ever since seeing The Wizard of Oz my imagination is apt to run away with me but in the case of Wankie it wouldn't be a yellow brick road we would follow, more likely some filthy mud track into the bush . . . lightning flashed non-stop, thunder loud enough to awaken the dead and then the electricity went off, the fans stopped turning and the floor of my office flooded. A messenger came in with a mop, another with a broom, and as fast as they pushed the water out more came in. I put my feet up on the desk and let them get on with it . . . I am told when the months of dry weather come along I shall yearn for the rainy season once more but as far as I can see the rains bring humidity and spread disease so there's not much of a choice between them. We are at the mercy of the elements.

5th March 1955

I am still busy with the Lepers. Yesterday we had a poor, sad man arrive. His fingers were all shrunk, nails disappeared completely. There is a Leprosarium at a place called Ngomahuru about five hundred miles away, I think I mentioned this before. I have to arrange for a special railway coach to take him there. It really is a horrible disease and the more I see of it the more I think of the book we all read, The story of a beautiful teenage debutante from New Orleans who was heartbreakingly diagnosed with leprosy, and entered the famous Carville hospital in Louisiana in the 1920s. Many of the patients changed their names to protect their families from the stigma attached to leprosy. Although she struggled most of her life with leprosy, now known as Hansen's disease, her secret could not be revealed. Neighbors of her family never knew what happened to her. About 20 years after she was diagnosed, Martin wrote her autobiography, 'Miracle at Carville', and it became a minor classic *. . . TB is also prevalent here though it appears we Europeans must be immune to it because we mix freely with the natives and one in ten of them are infected . . . I have been given yet another impossible task to fulfill. The natives in this part of the world have no idea how old they are and when a piccanin comes for a job he has to know approximately his age. Sooo . . . the messengers bring him in to the Nkosikas (Queen in Sindebele, that's me), and the Nkosikas looks them up and down and gives her opinion. Actually I can't tell the difference between a twelve year old and a fifteen year old. They have no idea of time at all — every day is much the same*

*as another . . . it doesn't make much difference any-
way — they get employed or married whatever age
they happen to be.*

✉

15 March 1955

*There are a tremendous amount of European cases
piled up. When we consider ourselves the 'superior
race' we should give it a bigger think! The main
troublemakers are the Afrikaans who seems to be
over-fond of assaulting both whites and blacks. To
assault a white isn't so bad but in the case of the
native; the poor bloke can't hit back and just has
to take all that is handed out to him before he can
complain to the police. Europeans are rarely put in
jail — nine times out of ten they get the option of a
fine and pay up willingly and then go off to commit another assault. There is definitely something
wrong with Rhodesian law and I doubt whether it
will change. If it does, it will probably be too late . . .
Last night we were sitting with friends when all of
a sudden we heard some awful moaning and groan-
ing. At first I thought it was some drunks coming
home after a party but then a messenger from the
hospital knocked on the door. A native had been
killed; doctor had to come right away. We came to
the conclusion that the noises we heard must be the
deceased's relatives. They chanted all night and I
nearly went round the bend. . . . there was another,
a European, killed in the mine the other day. What
a horrible job coal mining must be, safety doesn't
appear to be a priority.*

Accidents in the three working mines continued with an
average of at least one or more deaths a week. Though the

colliery is not under our jurisdiction, the NC's office issues the death certificates, and that means work for me: organizing, filling in forms and, if it's a European death, consoling the family. Often they're angry and let their frustrations out on me. All I can do is listen, commiserate and hand over the document they need.

And it isn't only down the mines where accidents happen, it is also on the slag heaps piled up around the mines where internal combustion confuses the Natives. These heaps are a colorful sight at night, but in the daytime they show no sign of danger. Children are fascinated: Why do they glow at night and not in the daytime? They climb onto the heaps, eager to find out what makes them glow in the dark, and every day one or two are treated for severe burns. Finally, we insisted a sign be erected, to read:

DANGER, INTERNAL COMBUSTION, DO NOT ENTER.

"Fat lot of use that is," Sherlock remarked. "How many of the Natives do you think can read? We need a guard there. Get on to the colliery and demand one."

"I think it would be better if you spoke to them."

"All right, get the manager on the phone — and by the way I'm the *Native* Commissioner, not the bloody European Supervisor."

"I just learned of another fatal accident, this time a European. The authorities are ordering an inquest. They should do the same for the Native miners — at least four of them are killed each month," I reported while dialing and not getting through.

Out of the blue, Sherlock asked, "What's all the hullabaloo going on in your office lately, wives and husbands at each other's throats?"

"I thought you'd be more distressed about the mine fatalities." I couldn't imagine why he'd suddenly come up with the subject of marriage.

"The mines are out of my jurisdiction. Put the phone down. I'll deal with them later." He started to go to his office, then turned and *asked again.* "What's causing all these marital problems?"

"It's the weather," Anderson deduced.

"Poppycock," Sherlock replied. "They marry for better or for worse, and they should stick to their vows."

Anderson piped up, "I'm staying single like you, Sherlock."

"Not that you have much of a choice around here, Anderson. Still, I'm curious about this lack of wedded bliss."

Listening to two bachelors giving their opinions on a matter neither of them had experienced, what can they possibly know?

"I do my best to calm them down. Perhaps it has something to do with the conditions in the mine — most of them are miners. Wives are scared, husbands hit the bottle. It's all related."

"The girl's a genius."

"No, I'm not. I'm married!"

That shut them both up.

So far, no guard at the slag heaps.

26th March 1955

I have joined the ranks of servant complaining Rhodesians. My cook refuses to work with Pashuni the new houseboy and I have no alternative other than to sack him. I certainly can't do without George — I wouldn't know what to do if we didn't have his cabbage staring us in the face every meal. George says Pashuni is cheeky but I think it is because they are both of different tribes and just don't get along. George is an Ndebele, Pashuni, a Chewa from Nyasaland. We may be 'federated' but that does not mean the natives have to love each other. Obviously they don't. Could be a problem looming somewhere on the horizon.

CHAPTER 19

It Takes All Sorts

I made a new friend, Betty, from Troon in Scotland, a teacher at the local non-denominational school. I invited her over for a cup of tea after we'd both finished work. Someone, not me, taught George to make scones and, though we needed a hatchet to break them apart, covered in butter and jam they weren't too bad.

Being a Scot, golf was Betty's game. At least it was until she came to Wankie, where she found putting greens were made out of coal slag. Though not internally combusting, it was a challenge she could do without. She decided to take up tennis, and that's where we met.

Betty became a frequent visitor to our home. When David had night duty, she'd stay over. Shortly before bedtime I'd find her brandishing a fly swat and holding a torch, searching for what she called "creatures of the night." She'd rather face the Loch Ness Monster than a giant hunting spider. After making sure we were safe from the larger insects, we'd crawl under the mosquito nets and chat.

"You must find your job interesting," she said in her quiet Scottish brogue.

"It's more than that, it's an education. You have no idea what the Natives get up to. It never ceases to amaze me."

"If you think the Natives are weird, let me tell you what happened in my class today — and they're all Europeans."

174

"Nothing terrible, I hope."

"No, just a bit unusual. A mother brought her son to enroll him in school. She spoke like a Glaswegian; they have quite a thick accent, even I find it difficult to understand them at times. She handed me her son's birth certificate, not sure why, still I glanced at it and handed it back. He was the right age for my class. The boy, eight years old, hung onto his mother for dear life. I thanked her and said her son would be fine with me. She gave him a hug in departure, as if he were going off to war.

"I seated the young lad and asked the rest of the class to welcome Guy and be nice.

"He put his hand up.

" 'What is it, Guy?' I asked.

" 'My name is GOOEY, not Guy.'

"Can you believe it? His mother must have seen the name written somewhere and pronounced it Gooey. What would you do? He can't spend the rest of his life being called Gooey."

"I don't know. If he likes being called Gooey, then I guess that's what you have to call him," I replied, hardly suppressing a giggle.

"Ach — I've had worse. In Scotland a wee thing came into class with an oversized name tag attached: Hamish Macduff Bruce Robbie Ewan Macpherson. His mother must have looked up every name in Scottish history and laden him with as many as she could get on the tag — thank God she'd left a few out. I asked him what he'd like to be called. He said, 'Bob!' "

It was then I promised myself, when we had children, I wouldn't embarrass them with names they couldn't remember or pronounce. David and I had been thinking of names for when the time came. In fact, we'd had a bit of a tiff about it. There were two women who'd been a major part of his early life, his mother, Violet, and his aunt, Fanny, both deceased.

"I have to respect them," said David.

"If you think I am going to name my daughter — "

"Our," he reminded me, "our daughter."

"Doesn't matter, I am not naming our child Violet Fanny."

"We have to use one of those names."

"Let's wait 'til the occasion warrants it. We could have a son." We put aside the naming of our unborn children.

The Head Teacher at the Wankie School insisted Betty inform Gooey's mother that her son's name was actually pronounced Guy. The mother, insulted and incensed, took the child out of Betty's class and sent him to the church school where the nuns didn't care what the child was called, as long as he prayed to Jesus and loved Mary.

And then we had the Methodist Church incident. Elias Postlethwaite was the pastor at the Methodist Church, a very tall, very skinny and very white, modern-day Uriah Heep. An unctuous married man with no children of his own, he held Sunday services and presided over funerals. He wasn't much in demand for weddings. His wife, wide of hip and not exactly an oil painting, conducted the choir.

It all came to a head when the mother of a ten-year-old brought her son to the police station, accusing the pastor of "meddlin' with me boy."

Monty lost no time in bringing the case to the Native Commissioners Office.

"Always knew there was something weird about him," Anderson remarked, having read the indictment aloud before handing it over to Sherlock.

"Sexual abuse of a minor — where's the bugger now?" Sherlock threw the indictment on my desk. He looked as if he was about to burst a blood vessel. "You're telling me they put a pedophile in charge of a Boy Scout outing?"

"It's the first complaint. I'm told he accompanied one of the Scouts' father's on an overnight to the game reserve," Monty replied. "Postlethwaite has not returned with them. He's missing."

"What do you mean, missing?

"Gone — left the camp before dawn. I went to the church to speak to his wife — she too has flown the coop. Told a friend she's going back to Manchester to see her sister."

"Good riddance to both of them. There are times I despair for the human race." Sherlock, enraged, paced the floor.

"What should I do with the complaint?" I inquired gingerly.

"Do? There's nothing we can do. Record it and hope a crocodile gets him."

Neither the pastor nor his wife was seen again in Wankie. His replacement arrived a month later, a young man straight out of an English divinity school, whose personality and fresh approach rejuvenated the church.

And then there was the unfortunate tale of the Police Chief Inspector's wife.

Mr. Calamas, the half Greek, half Italian owner of Calamas Everything Store in Wankie — in fact, the only store in Wankie — arrived and went directly to Sherlock to accuse the Chief Inspector's wife of stealing, "Every time she come to my shop, she no pay."

"Are you telling me she's a kleptomaniac?" Sherlock inquired.

"Klepto — I dunno — she a thief. I no more afford to feed the police lady."

Sherlock's door happened to be open; I couldn't help overhearing the conversation. He called me in, sat back in his chair and asked my advice. I had dealt with everything from bestiality to tribal differences. I had written marriage contracts and made out certificates for burials. This appeared to be more to do with diplomacy, something Sherlock didn't do well. I'd met the police lady when she came to get her driving licence — the second time — very friendly, very nice. Who would have thought there'd be a complaint made against her?

Sherlock asked if Calamas had proof.

"I see with'a my own eyes. She shops, she steal, she go. No money, no nuttin'. "

"If you press charges, in all likelihood her husband will have to leave the police force, and we don't want that."

"I don't'a care, I want'a my money. Natives don't'a pay me,

they don't'a come in'a my store no more. Police lady no pay me, she don't'a come in'a my store no more."

"Right. I will see that she does," Sherlock assured. "It's not that she can't afford it, it's more likely she's unaware of what's she's doing. Maybe a little . . . " He tried to think of a polite way to say the rest of the sentence, "Maybe she's a little not . . . not well in her head."

"I not'a well in my pocket. She no pay, she no more come in'a my store," Calamas repeated.

I came up with an idea. "Can you make a note of what she takes and send a bill?"

"Then you think she pay me?"

"Her husband, he will pay you."

Calamas thought for a moment. "I try — if no pay, she go to jail, right?"

"You will be paid," Sherlock stated, delighted the onus had been taken off him. "Brilliant, always knew it — takes a woman to come up with the right answer."

"Already I lose a lot'a money."

"Then add a bit to her bill each time, and you'll soon make it up. Mr. Calamas, your problem is solved. You will have your money, the Police Chief will stay in Wankie, and together we have solved the situation without upsetting the apple cart."

Calamas left scratching his head and probably thinking what on earth did billing a thief have to do with upsetting an apple cart?

29th March 1955

We have spent the day fishing in the Matetsi River — a tributary of the Zambezi, thirty five miles from Wankie. We caught a lot of fish and fried them on the spot for lunch — delicious and have enough to take home with us. I'm even more tanned than I was and now there isn't much to choose between me and an Indian. I wonder if I will ever acquire my English peaches and cream complexion again? It was extremely hot, must at least have been one hundred degrees, but lying under the shade of a Baobab tree waiting for the fish to bite, we didn't seem to notice it much. Fishing is a most restful pastime and we are going to do more of it. Whilst under the tree one of the fellows we were with pointed out a tree snake just coming out of a birds nest. By the look of it he had eaten its fill. We soon dispersed it by throwing stones. Where it went from there I don't want to know. I have an uncanny horror of snakes, in fact the very thought of them makes me shudder. Of course we were surrounded by monkeys and baboons which are cheeky but more or less harmless. Then a native boy decided to lead his herd of cows right where we were seated which was ridiculous as there were wide open spaces all around us. After shouting and waving him away he skillfully steered them pass, each one dropping a load of poop on its way. Then the flies descended and fishing was over for the day.

✉

2nd April 1955

We have an election coming off in Wankie in a couple of weeks and our office is the polling station so yours truly will be dragged in to count the votes — all two of them! I'm joking, probably a few more but not many of us are eligible to vote as we are not considered Rhodesian citizens — neither are the natives — if they were allowed to vote we'd be here till dooms day counting . . .

A friend of ours went down to Bulawayo the other day with strict instructions to get me a bottle of

"Light and Bright" — she arrived back with the sad news that Chemists no longer stock it because it explodes in the heat. I'll either have to stay out in the sun for hours or become a brunette.

An age old dispute between Africans living in two different kraals finally caused an uprising difficult to control. A ritual murder had taken place close to where these kraals were located. The police attributed the killing to the influence of the Mhondoros — women who played important roles in tribal life. They give advice, they heal and are highly respected. They are expected to perform miracles, but they also can cause problems. Troubled Africans go to them for advice and often wait for days in long lines for an audience. Mhondoros listen, chant, go into a trance and finally speak in the voice of the tribal spirit.

The chief of one kraal owned up to having his Mhondoro place a spell on the chief of the other. He instructed his Mhondoro to do likewise. Soon after, both chiefs reported their men were impotent and the females barren. Cattle grew thin and chickens stopped laying.

Murder? Well, that was a different category. Could that too be the work of the Mhondoros? Neither Mhondoro had committed the actual offense; they could not be charged with the crime.

The chiefs refused to cooperate with the police, they had done nothing wrong. All they had was a carved up body. The case was referred to the Native Commissioners Office. Sherlock, just returned from an ndaba in the Gwaai District, was not about to embark on another journey. Instead, he dispatched Ndozwi out to the troubled kraals to bring both Mhondoros back to speak with him.

A few days later Ndozwi returned with two very disgruntled Africans. Nomapitoli, the older woman, arrived in Native dress and shoeless. Sibongile, not young, not old, wore a moth-eaten blanket 'round her shoulders and a long piece of cloth reaching down to her bare feet.

"Do they know why they are here?" Sherlock asked.

"Yes, Nkos."

The two women stood away from each other, shouting and shaking their fingers at each other outside Sherlock's open door.

"That's enough! What are they saying? Interpret, Ndozwi, I haven't got all day," Sherlock demanded.

"They're fighting. They don't want to be here."

"The dead man, what about the dead man?"

"Nomapitoli says he was very bad. She does not know who killed him. She knows the Sangoma took his heart and buried it in the land. She makes medicines, not make murders."

"And the other one?"

"Sibongilis says Nomapitoli is wrong. Not the heart, Sangoma took his eyes. Bad man will not see where spirits take him."

"And did either of them have anything to do with the dead man?"

"No, Nkos."

"Did they know the dead man? How bad was he?"

"He took another man's wife. He took her baby girl child from Sibongilis kraal."

"Do we know where that child is?"

"No, Nkos."

"Did they have anything to do with this ritual murder?"

No, Nkos. Men kill, women are frightened of men. It is tribal, they have their own laws."

"Why am I here then? Why am I dragged into this rubbish?"

The women started yelling at each other again.

This was all new to me. Actually, everything that went on in the office had been, or was, new to me. These Mhondoros were from different kraals, they were known to be enemies, yet they stood firmly together, giving no clue that they knew anything about the murdered man.

Sherlock entered the room where the women were in my so-called office. "Not only do I have to prosecute everyday criminals brought before me by the police, now they try to involve me in the occult." He paced for a minute or so more before exploding with, "I've heard enough! Send 'em back, we're getting nowhere."

Sherlock stormed back into his office and slammed the door.

Ndozwi ushered the Mhondoros out, probably wondering why he'd spent three days in the bush looking for two stubborn women only to be told shortly after they'd arrived to take them back from whence they came.

Having witnessed the power of the two Mhondoros, I wanted to learn more. Sherlock suggested I meet with a Mhondoro named Kalowe, who he'd been told was a reasonably sane woman whose kraal was off the strip road that stretched north to the copper belt and south to Bulawayo.

"The most important powers are inherent in the Mhondoro's spirit. Kalowe is known to have the great ancestral spirit," Sherlock explained. "She is able to tell the future — she advises chiefs — she watches over her people. European judges and doctors are known to consult her. She must be treated with respect. I will not allow you to go alone; you'll need an interpreter. Take Ndozwi. Perhaps your husband will accompany you."

David said he had better things to do than consult a witch doctor.

"She's a Mhondoro — it's not same thing. She's possessed of a spirit. The spirit speaks through her. With doctors practice medicine, just like you."

"Portions of potions . . . they kill more than they cure!"

"I'm going."

"And if you don't come back, I'll understand you've been spirited away to live with the baboons in a cave somewhere."

"Stop it! Ndozwi's coming with me. I'll be fine."

"Why not Sherlock?" David asked.

"Someone has to look after the office. Anyway, he met this Mhondoro and said I should too."

"What is it with you people?"

"We, notice I said 'we,' are curious. We have a need to understand the people we help every day. Just because we're white doesn't mean we know it all."

I left early the next day. I drove, Ndozwi navigated.

Back on the Bulawayo-to-the-Falls strip road, trying to avoid the pot holes, watching out for elephant, we continued on for about forty miles without finding what we were looking for.

Eventually, Ndozwi recognized a clearing in the bush off the side of the road. "This is the place. We will have to walk."

I turned the car off the strips and parked it. We got out and began to walk.

A short way down a track cut through the bush, Ndozwi stopped to speak to an old man sitting under an acacia tree. "He say he is brother of Mhondoro. He say many important white people come to see her. She does not speak to everyone. He asks why you come."

"Tell him I want to meet her. I work with the Native Commissioner; she can help me understand the people I meet every day."

Ndozwi spoke to the old man.

The old man answered.

Ndozwi listened.

I waited.

Ndozwi interpreted. "He says Mhondoro is sleeping. When she wakes up he will speak to her. If she sees you, she has to dress — she is not dressed. You have to wait."

The old man saw the camera hanging from my shoulder and pointed to it. "No pictures." Obviously, he knew some words in English.

"How long does she sleep?" It was already noon, surely she'd wake soon.

Once again, Ndozwi spoke to the old man, the old man responded, and Ndozwi turned to me, saying, "He said he will let me know."

Ndozwi placed a blanket he'd brought along on the ground. "Sit, Medem."

There were large ant hills all around us. I declined his offer and went back to the car.

Ndozwi sat on his blanket. Knowing Africans had little awareness of time, there was no telling how long we'd be there. However, we were in luck.

An hour or so later her brother showed up and said, "The Mhondoro will see you now."

Her hut stood on an elevated mound made of ant heap. Men,

women and children sat silently nearby.

"Are they all here to see her?" I asked Ndozwi, who in turn asked the brother.

"They come every day to speak with the Mhondoro. They wait long time."

He took Ndozwi aside. It seemed an animated conversation. What were they talking about?

"You must take off shoes. You cannot speak until she is done. There are many who need her. You cannot stay long time. She is ready for you now."

I took off my shoes and I followed him into the hut. It was dark, very dark. Gradually my eyes adjusted. We sat on a ledge that circled the hut.

The Mhondoro, Kalowe, kneeled with her back to us. In one hand she held a rhinoceros horn, in the other a jug of water. She poured the water over the horn. The water fell into a tin basin beside her. She held the horn above her head and began to chant slowly, then a little faster, until the words tumbled together in a monotone. The shell shone like a beacon, an iridescent glow — her voice got stronger — the veins in her neck stood out. She continued to chant, and as suddenly as she began, she stopped and placed the shell in the tin basin. The light from the shell receded, to be replaced by a shard of sunlight coming through a crack in the mud wall of the hut, as if Kalowe had summoned a lighting expert.

She turned to face us. She spoke, Ndozwi interpreted:

"You may think you know why you are here. You do not. I have brought you to me to listen. I speak for the African people, the Mashonas and the Matabeles, those who are your servants. You will learn from the African people. Not the old ones who have no teeth, not the Africans who fight with stones and sticks, the Africans you teach your ways. You come because the spirits summoned you . . . you will leave . . . this is not your home."

"Tell her we are not all bad people. Many come to Africa to help."

"She says you come to Africa to take."

This was not going well. I had to try another tack. "Does she know where we work?"

"She knows. The Nkos is a good man — he does good work — he will die in Africa."

"And me?"

"You will go back where you came from. You will return to Africa, but you not stay."

"Tell her I do all I can to help the people who come to the Native Commissioners Office, but sometimes it is difficult."

"She says we do not speak the same language, do not have same spirits, we are not the same people."

"My husband is a doctor — he looks after African patients."

"She says, 'He treats the diseases you bring.'"

I could have argued with her on that but decided to stay quiet. She seemed to sense my hesitancy.

"The doctor cannot do what the Sangoma does."

Kalowe the Mhondoro

There wasn't much more to be said. I could feel the spirit leaving her. She sank to the ground. The shard of light disappeared. We were alone in the darkness of her hut. My meeting with Kalowe the Mhondoro had ended.

"Wait, we cannot leave, she must tell us when to go." Ndozwi advised. Kalowe slowly came to, she sat up and spoke directly to Ndozwi.

"She says you will now take her photo."

And I did — then stepped outside into the brilliant sunshine.

Many more Natives had gathered. They stared at me. They made me feel uneasy.

On the way back I asked Ndozwi how Kalowe could possibly know so much about me.

"The spirit speaks for her — not Kalowe who speaks."

"I don't think she liked me," I mumbled.

Ndozwi, the diplomat, ignored my assumption.

That evening, sitting with David in our breezeway, he asked me about my day.

"It's hard to describe my encounter with Kalowe. All I can say is I met a wise woman who spoke to me. When I grasp what I experienced I'll be able to speak about it. Right now, I'm not really sure what actually happened."

Soon it will be my 21st birthday.

In London I'd have celebrated it with old friends and family at a hotel or a nice restaurant. In Wankie we have new friends, and David considers the dogs family. There is a beer-reeking, 1930s shack they call The Baobab Hotel, where only drunks and prospectors gather, which is definitely not for me. Then there's the Mine Club, but they're a snooty lot and most of them old enough to be my parents. I asked George if he had any suggestions.

"Medem — we have breivleis."

Once again I had to ask, "What's that?"

"We dig a hole in the ground, we put wood and coal in it, we light it, and when it is very hot, we cook meat and boerewors and mealies."

I knew boerewors to be sausage and mealies corn on the cob. I'd let George set the menu.

25th April 1955

We will be having about forty people to the party which we hope to hold outside with a barbecue, or as they call it here, a breivleis. The rainy season will be over by then so we won't have to be worry about the heavens wrath. Fancy spending ones 21st in the bl----y bundu — most normal people celebrate at some select place in town — but not me — I have to be different . . . yes, in answer to your question, there are some awful diseases in our part of Africa and I could get malaria, bilharzias, leprosy, black water fever, typhoid, yellow fever, tetanus, tuberculosis, dengue fever, cholera, etc., etc., We take Paludrine to counteract malaria, we don't go swimming in strange rivers to get bilharzia, I haven't been in close contact for any length of time with a leper, black water fever died out a few years ago, typhoid has its outbreaks but we've been inoculated and also again tetanus and yellow fever — does that put your mind at rest, Mummy . . .

Nurses, doctors, all of the staff at the Native Commissioners Office, including the District Commissioner, a few acceptable from the colliery — forty people in all came on Sunday to celebrate with me. I was still the kid in the crowd, but I'd reached a milestone.

David presented me with two black, mixed-breed puppies. One would have been enough, we already have two dogs the size of small ponies. I'm thinking of opening a kennel. Bianca made me a birthday cake. Ned Sherlock gave me a carved ivory box. I'd been given enough books to open a library, and we all enjoyed the breivleis.

The rainy season has come to an end. We ate under the clear African sky, with stars it seemed we could reach out and touch, while the upside-down moon shone down on us. We remained outside after our guests left; it was a beautiful night. We stayed in the shadow of the rondavels, the embers of the fire glowing and the drums from the compound seeming to keep time with the beating of my heart. I looked back on my first twenty-one years. Years made up of war, shelters, and bombs, years of rationing and shortages, years of recovery and slow growth and now nearly a year of living in Africa. The very best year of all spent in a place called Wankie in The Federation of Rhodesia and Nyasaland. The land where my husband's relatives pleaded with him not to take me, certain I would perish. Where they said only prospectors and out of work Brits go, where the trains don't run and roads don't exist. They were wrong. Perhaps they were mixing us up with Australia — though they left out convicts, so maybe not.

And the fact is I feel very much alive. I wouldn't want to be anywhere else. Yes, I complained about the rain and the climb up the kopje and the practical jokes, and I still can't fathom why they continued to use tar on the road outside our door, because it melts and lands up at the bottom of the road and has to be picked up to be used for the same purpose the following day; or why the garden boy insists on washing the car in the rain; and, why we don't have a local dentist, causing me to drive two hundred miles south to find one. Not to mention the primitive living quarters, which we share with insects and lizards and chameleons and spiders and scorpions and the occasional snake. None of it would I exchange for a mundane existence in a London suburban setting.

The townies can keep their posh houses and numerous servants. At the ripe old age of twenty-one, I feel I am where I am supposed to be — in this unrelenting, not very beautiful, often intriguing, close to one of the wonders of the world, elephant domiciled, baboon overloaded, coal producing, British outpost on the Continent of Africa.

4th May 1955

Look at the date — today is my real birthday. "I'm twenty one today, twenty one today, I've got the key of the door, never been 21 before," actually I don't have the key, we haven't got one. Can't say I feel any different to how I felt yesterday. I looked in the mirror this morning to see if I could find any wrinkles on my visage but all I could see were hundreds of freckles which I am pleased to say ain't the sign of old age only a sign of the merciless African sun. So I've reached the age of discretion and will now have to start behaving myself — what a 'orrible thought. When we meet again I doubt whether you will find much change in me unless of course wrinkles have begun to develop by then . . .

31st May 1955

. . . at the moment there is a smallpox scare throughout the many kraals in our district and the various health officers are working overtime trying to vaccinate the natives who are not being co-operative. By the way I have become a blood donor, might as well do something to earn my keep and perhaps save somebody's life. Black or white, I'm not fussy. It's strange we can use white man's blood for Africans but never ever vice versa . . . did I tell you about the European foreman who had a glass eye and needed to leave his miners for a while. He knew if they saw him leave they would stop what they were doing so he took out his glass eye and left it on a post in the mine. 'Alright' he said 'this eye will watch you while I'm away' and he left. The boss boy looked at the eye, looked at his fellow workers, took off his hat, covered the eye and they all lay down and went to sleep.

Sherlock called a meeting. I took notes.

"I've been informed we're surrounded by herds of elephants," said Sherlock. "We are not allowed to kill or harm them in any way, although I have suggested a cull to the authorities to control the situation. I am tired of being cut off halfway through a telephone conversation because one or more of them have knocked down our telephone poles. It's not just my inconvenience, it's the fact they are stripping the leaves off the trees, as well as knocking them down. We need trees and bush to secure the ground. We have to find a way to discourage them and keep them in the game reserve, and we must stop poachers killing them for the ivory. Hunters who apply for a licence are allowed only one elephant. The hunter must give the meat of the elephant to the Natives he takes with him on the hunt and pay ten shillings for their labor."

"Who gives the culling order?" Nicholson asked.

"That will have to be the government. I imagine we're talking about quite a number. Don't like the thought of it, but we have to be sensible."

They jabbered on for an hour without coming up with any other solution of how to keep the elephants away from Wankie.

I had other things on my mind — there was nothing I could do about elephants, but a lot I could do about the state of my underwear.

4th June 1955

Mummy darling, I am in need of underwear! I think mine has given in because the washer woman takes it down to the river and scrubs everything we wear with a stone. I've asked her to wash our clothes in the bath tub but she refuses saying 'not good, no clean' so I walk around with holes in my knickers. I also need slips and cotton nighties. I'm thinking of going into the lingerie business — I'll pay you for the items . . . though on second thoughts I really don't have the time to become a retailer so just make me proud of my undergarments and I'll wash them by hand in the future.

11th June 1955

Yesterday we went to a clinic held ten miles away from Wankie. The really raw native from the Zambezi dressed in beads and string attended — it was something out of a travelogue. Women with sticks through their noses and witch doctor marks all over them — little children hiding never having seen a white man before. Their diseases are numerous and pitiful — scabies, yaws and nearly everyone with a venereal disease in one stage or another. And what happens, they get an injection of penicillin, it clears up and in a few weeks time they are just as sick as they were when the doctor first sees them. They all have vitamin deficiency and their span of life is short, so sad. It will take many years before all these different tribes are rounded up and taught what we consider hygiene — I doubt whether it will be in my lifetime or my children's come to that.

A week later a messenger came to our door late in the evening with a note from Delaney: "Train crash along the new line being cut through the bush. Bring medical supplies."

David handed the note to me and rushed to get dressed.
"I'm going with you."

"Won't be a pretty sight. We'll have to stop off at the hospital. I'll run in, pick up morphine, syringes, bandages, you stay in the car, keep the engine running. Damn thing's been stalling."

We followed a rough path that had been cut through the

bush and after a very bumpy journey found our way to the site where hurricane lamps lit up a scene of pandemonium. Africans from nearby kraals helped passengers from the twisted carriages. Sisters from the hospital attended the injured. A lorry stood by to take them to the hospital. Ten bodies were laid out beside the railway track.

I looked over to where the train driver was sitting. His right leg was covered in blood seeping from a deep wound just above the knee. Delaney was holding him down while Sister Mary tried to stem the bleeding.

"It's his bloody fault, drunk as a lord," said the Sister.

David went over to them and gave the driver a shot of morphine, "Be a miracle if we save his leg. Get him into the lorry immediately."

"The European ambulance should be here any minute." Sister Mary advised.

"For Christ's sake, this isn't the time for separating the races!" David shouted.

"It certainly is not, but we can't just throw him in with a load of Natives. He needs immediate attention, and that lorry will wait around until it's full. I have little sympathy for the man, but we cannot let him bleed to death."

"Someone should inform Welensky," David said.

"And how do you think I'd be able to manage that with all this going on?" Sister demanded.

Soon after, I found out Roy Welensky was Minister of Transport. (He became the Prime Minister of The Federation of Rhodesia and Nyasaland in 1956.)

"He'll know soon enough. Now you just get on with treating the wounded, and I'll take care of getting them out of here as quickly as I can."

Sister Mary Ellen had more important concerns to worry about.

There were injured women with babies strapped to their backs, old men hobbling, young men crying, David rushing between the injured, me consoling, Delaney swearing, and the Sisters run off their feet. The colliery sent another lorry full of miners to help clear the line, only recently installed.

16th June 1955

. . . if anyone would have told me a year ago that I could console a dying man with an eye hanging out of his badly crushed head without fainting I'd have thought them crazy. I stayed with him, holding his hand and then when no more could be done I moved on. It's amazing what you can tolerate when it's a case of having to. We stayed 'til sun up by which time the dead were still being identified and the injured taken to hospital. Wankie is in shock and there will be many repercussions from this accident and probably a lot of work for me.

On a lighter note we have both become members of the Wankie Golf Club. At the moment I'm not that enthusiastic about the game but I understand it gets you eventually then you never want to give up. The course isn't at all like the one behind our house in Woodside Park. If you should happen to hit too far off the ball goes in to the bush amidst the elephants and snakes and even the cost of the ball isn't enough incentive to make people go to look for it. And as for the balancing rocks — if you hit them the ball ricochets back and can easily knock you out. I think I'll stick to tennis . . . After many delays the new hospital is finally completed and we are invited to a roof wetting given by the contractors.

Sherlock barged into my office with the invitation in his hand. "It's not finished."

"It is. We received the same invitation," I said.

"The European wing is finished, the African section is not. Have you seen where those poor buggers have to seek medical attention? It's a travesty. We should boycott this party. Let them celebrate when the entire facility is open. I'm the Native Commissioner, for God's sake. I can't be seen there. I'd be a complete hypocrite if I attended."

"Oh, never gave it a thought. I suppose I should stay away too."

"Let your conscience be your guide."

As the wife of the doctor, I had to accept. As the Clerk of the Court, I ought to refuse. But this was Rhodesia — Natives were second class citizens. Obviously, their needs would be second to ours.

Sherlock represented the Africans in the Matabele Province. Occasionally his path crossed with the colliery. A good example: the railway accident. But then we all got involved with that.

The railways held an inquest. The driver of the train faced charges of culpable homicide, drinking while in charge of a train and reckless behavior. The colliery cleared the line and soon had the freight wagons, filled with coal, rolling again.

Had we requested the Native Hospital to be completed at the same time as the European one, it would have fallen on deaf ears. The colliery provided medical facilities for Europeans and Africans. Without the European staff there would be no coal output; therefore, the European hospital had preference over the Native one.

Before the colliery, the Africans had no medical facility other than ill-equipped clinics. With the colliery they at least had an outdated hospital that might eventually be replaced. Until then, the Native hospital dealt not only with the patient but also with his family, who came along with him, causing overcrowded conditions in the wards. Often there were more Natives sleeping on the floors and in the corridors than in the beds, and even if they were told to leave they came back. The area outside the hospital was equally unruly, crowded with villagers, friends and family of the patients, all chanting, crying and cooking their meals on wood fires.

I accompanied my husband to the Roof Wetting Party — he insisted I go. A few dignitaries and the usual set of colliery husbands and wives were there, along with numerous unidentified people. It hardly mattered whether I attended or not.

Sherlock, on the other hand, was conspicuous by his absence.

Two new doctors came on board: one a trained surgeon, Dr. Theron, the other, Dr. Adams, a radiologist brought in along with the new x-ray equipment. Medically, things were looking up in Wankie, at least, if you happened to be white.

David's surgery days were over, and he couldn't be happier.

20th June 1955

We attended the roof wetting party at the new hospital which will be the best equipped European hospital in the Federation of Rhodesia and Nyasaland and as half of Wankie seems to enjoy bad health they will make good use of it. Even the native unfinished part of it will be more than acceptable although the general agreement is 'it is far too good for them.' Don't for one minute think I agree with the white overlords, as far as I am concerned they should hold their tongues and be thankful they have cheap labor. They should also treat them better. Have they ever given a thought to what it would be like without their help? I think not . . . Europeans here would be lost without native help — who would do the scut work then? Surely not us!

Yesterday we went up to the golf club for a cool drink and listened to the conversations. All we could hear was talk about birdies, bogies and handicaps — we just looked blank. No doubt in a few weeks time, if we decide to learn the game, we'll know what they are talking about. Incidentally that place would close down if it wasn't for the natives. They are the caddies, the kitchen workers, the gardeners, the bathroom cleaners, the run and fetch it goers . . . and I could go on but have to get on with my work which has everything to do with them and very little to do with us.

CHAPTER 20

Murder Most Foul

It was Tuesday morning and Native Court day. Natives filled the courtroom, the accused came in led in by two Native policemen. I sat with my notepad, ready to take down the proceedings.

This was a murder case. Panyesani Mngange had taken an axe and lodged it in Longwe Ndole's head. Longwe had stolen three chickens and given them as a gift to his intended in-laws. The in-laws refused to return the chickens. Panyesani sought revenge. Obviously, there was no defendant, only disgusting photographs of the dead man with an axe stuck in the middle of his head. His relatives and members of his kraal were present, seeking justice.

Sherlock was nowhere to be seen. A messenger handed me a piece of paper. A note read: *Can't take court today, tummy got the collywobbles. Ned*

I had to be very careful here. I didn't want to cause a riot. I stood up and slowly walked to the bench. I summoned Ndozwi to interpret for me. I whispered, "Tell all those present there is a problem."

"What kind of problem, Medem?"

"Not so loud — Master Sherlock is sick."

"He going to die?"

"Of course not — just not well enough to hold Court."

"They will think he make excuse. We must find a doctor to tell them."

"That's ridiculous."

"It is not. I tell them, they don't believe me. They say it is a European story, make them keep coming back."

"Then send a messenger to the hospital and get a doctor."

And we sat, all of us, in a steaming, smelly courtroom awaiting the arrival of a doctor. I prayed it wouldn't be my husband.

An hour later Dr. Delaney arrived, dressed in white shorts, white shirt, white socks and white shoes. No one could mistake his profession. "I have better things to do than come up here because Sherlock has a tummy ache. Where is he?"

"He's home. All you have to do is tell the Natives in the courtroom you have examined the magistrate, who is not well, and they should come back on Thursday when he'll be better."

"Do they also need a diagnosis?" Delaney asked sarcastically.

"No, they need to be reassured."

"Sounds like a load of ballyhoo to me."

"Please, just do it."

Delaney stood beside Ndozwi and addressed the Natives: "The boss Magistrate is very sick. He will get better. There will be no evidence given today."

A lot of *ahhhhhhs* and grunts sounded through the court.

The defendant left the same way he came in.

"I'm sure all Sherlock has is a hangover. It will be gone by tomorrow, and he'll be fine by Thursday," Delaney said, sweating profusely. "I need this like a hole in my head. I'll send one of the new doctors up for the next session, let him see what goes on here." He mumbled a few profanities directly at the Natives as he left.

The Africans in the courtroom would not budge. They just sat there.

"Move them out, Ndozwi." I was startled by my unusually firm words.

"No, Medem, they say they will stay 'til Nkos comes back."

"They can't."

"I move them, they come back. They have blankets and food, they stay."

"Tell them this is not a hotel."

And stay they did until the next Native Court day, when they all filed back to the court from where they had camped for two days under the jacaranda tree outside my office.

Sherlock, his dog following, settled on the bench, seemingly recovered from what ailed him. He banged the gavel on his roughly hewn desk.

"God save the Queen."

Sherlock looked up from his notes. "Panyesani Mngange is remanded to the High Court in Bulawayo."

And that was that.

Why he couldn't have said that on the day of Panyesani's first arraignment, I could not fathom, and by the sound of the uproar in the courtroom, neither could the relatives and friends of the murdered victim.

"God save the Queen."

Sherlock gathered up his papers and walked out.

I was left with an angry mob. They'd hung around for two days, and now they'd have to find a way to get to Bulawayo. Their spokesman came up to me as I prepared to leave my office on the second day. He spoke English.

"We want bus to Bulawayo."

"There is no government bus to Bulawayo," I answered. "And it will be a long time before the case comes up in front of the High Court."

"He killed my brother."

"He will be in prison. You will receive justice." I couldn't think of anything better to say.

Sherlock came to my rescue.

"Close up and go home. The Natives appear restless."

"They are."

"I mean it. Close the office. Now."

Back in my rondavel — we'd decided to give the huts, their proper name — I wrote home leaving out the reason for my afternoon off.

◻

25 th June 1955

We had our first round of golf today and managed to lose four balls. It isn't half as easy as it looks and it will be many a moon before we can play with any-one — that is if we continue to play what appears to me to be a suicidal endeavour. It isn't an easy course; the putting greens are made of coal slag. A rake is provided to flatten out what the golfer has indented, the trouble being every time you make a foot print you have to rake and that means you're raking more than playing. That's why we have a caddie. Then there are the balancing rocks — hit one of those and the balls comes right back, usually hitting some part of your anatomy. One landed on my nose and now it has a rather large bump. Real golfers on the tee behind wait impatiently for you to move on. The golfers in front have to spend time raking and while you wait your turn the mopani flies attack. By the time you get to the 9th hole you are ready for a stiff drink and as I only imbibe Coler tonic and lemonade it has little effect on my state of mind anyway there are no refreshments at the 9th hole — you have to plod on to the 18th. Added to these frustrations if you happen to come across an elephant he has right of way and if your ball lands in an elephant's foot print you are allowed to pick it up and move it, (not the elephants foot, the ball!) We have to avoid snakes, baboons, and other wildlife. Golf is not a game here in Wankie — it's a dangerous obstacle course. By the way the cad-dies name for golf is 'ikona bonieelee' — translated means 'I cannot find the ball.'

Okay, it wasn't collywobbles, it was jaundice. The day after the hearing, Sherlock turned yellow.

Anderson took charge.

Lots of Chinese jokes were going around. I carried on with my work, there was still plenty to do. An Assistant Magistrate was due in on the evening train, the same train that would take Panyesani to his pre-destined demise. I wished he, the Magistrate, were here, because an African had just come into the office holding his left hand in his right hand. I mean literally holding it. His shirt and trousers were covered in blood.

"Medem, I go fishing — crocodile bite off my hand. He drop my hand. I pick it up."

"Oh, my God!" I screamed. "Stay there, don't move." I called for a messenger. The only one who ever answers me is Ndozwi. He came.

"That man bleeding," he said.

"I can see that!" I yelled. "That man has to go to the hospital now, right now! I can't leave the office. You must take him."

"I not drive," Ndozwi exclaimed.

"Find a sheet, find something. He's about to faint. So am I. Go find Mr. Anderson. Now, Ndozwi, NOW!"

I cut off a sleeve of his shirt and used it as a tourniquet, tying it as tightly as I could. I wrapped his wrist with bandages from our first aid kit. I looked around to find something to place the severed hand in, could only find a wastepaper basket so in it went. Ndozwi came back with Anderson, and together they lifted the man off the floor and ran with him to the waiting Land Rover.

I telephoned the main hospital to let them know a serious case was on the way, and they should be ready. "A Native has had a serious accident, he cannot wait, he has to be seen right away."

"This is the European Hospital."

"Then put me through to the Native Hospital"

"There is no telephone at the Native Hospital."

"Send a runner — this is an emergency."

"I'll put you onto a nurse who may be able to help you. Who

is this man?" And she began to ask a number of questions.

I interrupted her. "Listen, I don't know his name! I have not seen his situpa! I have no idea how old he is! All I know is his left arm is a bleeding stump! The hand is in a wastepaper basket, and if you don't get a doctor to see him immediately, he will bleed to death!"

"European or Native?" she asked.

"Oh, for God's sake, he's a human being and he's on his way to you!" I yelled.

Did they, the contractors, ever think of adding a telephone line to the new Native Hospital, if and when it was completed? And if they had, would there be a connection when that hospital was completed?

I'd just attended a lavish affair to celebrate the opening of the European Hospital and this poor man would probably be shunted to the Native Hospital because he was black, while the best, up-to-date medical facility in Southern Africa sat half empty.

Sherlock had a good reason for not attending the Roof Wetting Celebration, and this incident proved him right.

28th June 1955

Exactly a year has now gone by since we left the shores of England and so much has happened in that time. As I look back it all seems like a wonderful dream. Our first year of married life has been the happiest anyone could wish for and I only wish the rest of our lives together will be spent in the same harmony. We have covered over ten thousand miles and visited many lands and yet, in our heart, certainly my heart, England calls us back. It is where we want to settle and raise our family. Africa is full of thrills and strange primitive people but unless one has the pioneer spirit strongly instilled it is only a way to live for a short spate of time. From North Africa, East, South and Central it all totes up to the same ever present conflict between black and white, and, as I have said so many times before, I'd sooner read about it in the daily papers than continue to take an active part. Our first year has taught me a great deal; to tolerate and appreciate others way of life. Europeans who have lived here many more years than us don't want things to change, they are comfortable being waited on, lording it over those less fortunate, taking for granted and thinking it's their right to demand obedience. The Native Affairs department has been an eye opener. We should have a slogan written on our door saying 'We Care' — But as much as we care and do all that we can to help the natives, it will never be enough — they need so much and we Europeans can give so little. I know it will all come to a head one day — the natives will no longer put up with us — they will demand respect — refuse to work for a pittance and revolt. I don't want to be here to take sides because the side I would take would not be that of the big boss overseer.

CHAPTER 21

Take a Seat

I'd written a somewhat righteous and serious letter and felt very good about it. My satisfaction was soon curtailed by the sound of a car dragging its front end up the kopje. It parked outside the Native Affairs Department. A distraught, middle-aged man shouted for someone to get him out. Messengers came to his rescue and with great difficulty managed to pull the driver's door open. The man eased himself out, brushed himself off and limped into my office.

"What happened?" I asked.

"What happened, I'll tell you what happened. I was driving the strip road from Bulawayo, hoping to get to the Falls in time for lunch, when about half a dozen elephants walked across the road. So, I stopped to let them pass. They lolloped their way slowly into the bush and disappeared — all except one, that is. He just stood there, wouldn't move. I waited. He waited. I gave him time. He wouldn't budge. I honked the horn and then, well, you won't believe this, he turned 'round, took a good look and placed his rear end on the front of my car and sat down. The bonnet slowly caved in. One of the herd came back, took a look around, put his or maybe her trunk on the seated elephant, as if to say, "Get up." And he did — leaving me flabbergasted and not knowing what to do. I was afraid to get out of the car and then found out even if I wanted to I couldn't. I turned on the engine and, to my amazement, the car started."

Sherlock came out of his den. "Aha. I learned long ago never to honk the horn of a car near elephants, it mimics their mating call. What happened to you, old chap, is your elephant thought you were trying to get off with him. Never actually seen one of them fall in love with a Volkswagen. Congratulations, you've made the record books."

"You shitting me?"

"I beg your pardon."

"Look at my car — what am I supposed to do?"

"Just be thankful the engine's at the back — you'd still be stuck in the bush if it weren't."

Sherlock left to examine the car. He wasn't the only one interested, a crowd of Africans surrounded it, and Anderson and the Land Development Officer were out there laughing hysterically.

"I'm glad they all find this amusing. Damned if I do."

The owner of the car needed advice, sympathy, and he wasn't getting it from them. I offered him a drink. "A cup of tea? A glass of water?"

". . . a beer would be nice."

"Sorry, we don't keep liquor here," which was a bald-faced lie since they all had a flask of something hidden away in their desks.

"Water, then. I'll get a drink when I get this mess sorted out."

Sherlock returned. "I suggest you get back in your vehicle and coast to the police station halfway down the kopje. They have a mechanic there. The messengers can give you a push. Doubt whether much can be done with it, though. Sorry, old man — at least you'll know what not to do next time you have a face on with elephants. Give our lovely lady clerk your name — she'll enter it in the record book just in case I need to refer to it one day."

"Arnold Rothstein, I'm a traveling salesman. Now I'll be a walking salesman by the look of it."

"Don't you have insurance?"

"I do. Perhaps you'd like to take them on. I can just hear it when I report this. 'Sorry, old boy, we don't insure against elephants.' "

I had the distinct impression Sherlock would be dining out on this one for years to come. Why he came to us, I'll never know, but then there were many who came to us who weren't Africans. After a while I gave up even trying to find out. Apparently, the salesman also gave up — his car remained in its sorry state at the police station, and then one day it disappeared. It was found a few weeks later in the Native compound — seats and engine removed, and someone had taken up residence in it.

✉

1st July 1955

We met His Excellency the Governor of Rhodesia on Monday night and chatted with him for a short while. Nice enough fellow who seemed agreeable and pleasantly surprised about Wankie. Seems we have a bad name for some reason or other, though if you ask me it has a lot to do with the climate. It happens to be the hottest place in the Federation — on the other hand it is on the boundaries of the Game Reserve so if you overlook the smoke stacks of the colliery, and the one road, and the dubious population, then perhaps it isn't such a terrible place. When I come home I'll tell you the tale of a man in a car facing an elephant, you won't believe it but it's true . . .

Sherlock has gone on a two-week holiday, but I'm not allowed to. Well, I could take time off, but the locum Native Commissioner informed me that, if I did, I'd forfeit all forthcoming pay increments. That's government for you — they offer with one hand and take away with the other. The increments were probably miniscule, but added to that, because I signed on for a year, I would have to sign on for another year should I decide to take a holiday. There is absolutely no logic to any of this.

The Colonial Service has the most ridiculous rules, but then no one stays in it for very long, so what the heck. Our ever decreasing empire may have something to do with it.

"What have you decided to do?" Anderson inquired.

"Stay," I replied.

"Good. Got a job for you! Chief Wange tells me his herd boy is having an affair with his cow — he didn't actually say it that way, but that's what he's on about. You can either talk to the herd boy or the Chief. What's your preference?"

"I'll talk to the cow!"

"Oh, for God's sake . . . "

I learned more than I wanted to know that day.

2nd July 1955

A four-day holiday is coming up and we're off to Livingstone this weekend to do some shopping. As you know they take our clothes down to the river and scrub them with a rock which leaves them in terrible shape. When I speak to our washer lady about it she says 'bad cloth' I think those are the only words she knows in English. Livingstone's not exactly a metropolis but it has more shops than we do, all run by Indians. Mind you having more shops isn't difficult — remember we only have one and that's mainly grocery. Won't be surprised if I come back wearing a sari and smelling of curry. Tata for now.

It is Rhodes and Founder's Weekend, commonly referred to as Rogues and Scroungers, time to celebrate the life of Cecil Rhodes. Not sure we should be doing that, although he did discover this amazing land. I suppose we should be grateful. The office is to be closed for four days. That's what I am grateful for. Sherlock will be back in charge, which is just as well. His replacement has no sense of humour and therefore is far too stern for us. We needed a bit of levity in our jobs. If we take it too seriously, we'll probably land up in the loony bin.

✉

4th July 1955

We needed a few things at the shops, so we didn't stop to see the Falls immediately, but went straight to Livingstone. Our luck didn't hold, since we found the shops all shut. David surprised me and arranged for me to take my first plane ride yesterday. We took off from a little airfield near Livingstone in a two-seater Cessna to fly over the Victoria Falls. David awaited his turn on the ground. It is even a more wonderful site from the air and now we have seen the Falls from every conceivable angle from the Southern Rhodesia side and the Northern Rhodesian. From the air it is an awesome experience. Rainbows arch over gushing, falling water. A flat seemingly calm Zambezi river suddenly plunges into cataracts and becomes a white foaming mass. The rainbows seemed to touch the bottom of the plane. We could recognise the rapids. And this is our dry season — perhaps not the best time to view what we are told is even more spectacular when the rains come. It is one and half times the size of Niagara Falls. Little wonder Livingstone was humbled in its presence when he came across them in 1885. So am I in 1955. Above the Falls on either side of the

Zambezi there is dense tropical vegetation. As the river winds its way it runs through rugged mostly uninhabited terrain. Flying not too high we saw hippos and crocodiles seemingly oblivious of where the water they frolic in is about to cascade over the rocks so close by. Wait a moment, don't think hippos or crocs frolic — more likely waiting for some tasty morsel to come their way. I remembered the sign I'd seen when we first arrived — 'bathing is suicidal' — these creatures have been known to add us to their daily menu.

On my return I had to speak to the Chief about his herd boy — me being the lowest on the totem pole and no one else volunteering, I had no choice.

Ndozwi interpreted.

"The cow not giving milk," he said.

"What has that got to do with the herd boy?" I asked.

"A headman saw him doing bad things to the cow."

"Like what?"

"I cannot tell you, Medem."

"Then why are we having this conversation?"

"We are having conversation because Chief Wange wants herd boy arrested."

"Then he should go to the police."

"He frightened of police."

"Tell him to give the herd boy a different job."

"He says he not from his kraal."

"Then send him back to his own kraal."

"The chief says not good idea."

"Why?"

"He promised in marriage to girl from his kraal."

"So, make him marry the girl. Tell the Chief he'll be better when he's married and he won't need to do bad things to the cow."

"The Chief says he likes your idea. He will see if cow gives milk after herd boy is married. He come back let you know."

"I'd prefer he didn't."

Ndozwi was wise enough not to interpret my last remark. He escorted the Chief out of the office, and so ended the strange story of the Chief and his herd boy.

✉

7th July 1955

. . . the budget for the year has just been announced. Cigarettes have gone up a lot — they are now a shilling a hundred and everyone is moaning. Can you imagine what they would say if they had to pay the English price for cigarettes. Rhodesia is a tobacco producing country, in fact it is its main crop and we all feel guilty if we don't smoke. I'm not a heavy smoker — probably wouldn't smoke at all if wasn't for keeping up the economy . . . so what with being a non drinker and a more or less non-smoker I can't really in all honesty call myself a true Rhodesian. There is one thing I can say that I like about cigarettes — that's the box they come in — I mean the Rothman's thirty box because I can make notes on the back of it without searching around for a piece of paper when I'm out of the office.

A European hunter came into my office holding a very large brownish snake — I remembered the other time this happened. Why do they think we knew anything about snakes? I ran out the door, leaving the idiot holding the wiggling creature.

Sherlock heard the commotion and came to see what was going on.

I peered through the open window. I was not about to go back until the man and his snake had gone.

"I don't see any sign anywhere saying, 'Bring in your snake,'" Sherlock remarked, looking around to see if there were a sign.

"This is the Native Commissioners Office. We deal with people, not snakes."

An explanation came forth, but I couldn't hear what the snake man said. I called one of the messengers.

"The snake bite him — he ask if it poison."

Sherlock grabbed the Native and the snake, shoved both in the Land Rover, and off he drove like a maniac down the kopje to the hospital.

Ndozwi found the incident amusing.

I did not.

✉

21st July 1955

. . . they are just playing on the radio Brahms Lullaby and it takes me back to the war years when the whole family were boarded out with Grandpa and Grandma after they were bombed out in Aldgate and Uncle Sid gave them his house in Poynings Way. And even there the bombs fell fast and furious and no one knew from one moment to the next whether they'd live to see the light of another day — you and Aunty Hetty in unison hummed the cradle song no doubt with your hearts in your mouths but nevertheless comforting we frightened children. Isn't it strange the way certain melodies bring to mind memories you wish to forget but never go away.

Ndozwi came in with a live chicken, flapping its wings and making a hell of a noise in its efforts to be set free.

"Chicken you ordered from butcher, Nkosikas," he announced in regal tones.

"Take that creature out of here."

"Medem, this is the chicken you order. Butcher wants you to see it before he kills it."

"I want a dead chicken, de-feathered, gutted and ready for the oven."

Sherlock came out of his office. "Why are you holding a chicken, Ndozwi?"

"It's for the medem, sir."

"I don't want it. I want a dead chicken, not a live one."

Sherlock instructed Ndozwi to take it to his cook, and he left with the chicken still squawking loudly.

"I can't eat anything I've seen alive and running around."

"How do you think we get our chickens?" Sherlock asked. "They all come this way from Bulawayo. The railway refrigeration containers often break down; butchers can't take a chance."

"You've put me off chicken for the rest of my life."

"Nonsense, you and David will join me for a delicious meal this evening."

During dinner, Sherlock let David know my overreaction to the flapping chicken and should have left it at that; instead, he went on to say everything we eat — be it meat, chicken or fish — all of them lived, breathed and pooped. He could have left out the last description. I considered claiming vegetarian status as I had with Bianca and the brains she served the first time we had dinner in Madumabisa.

30th July 1955

. . . I am alone under the mosquito net. On one side I have the gun, on the other side a good book to read after I've finished this epistle. The dogs are sleeping peacefully in the breeze-way . . . I think it will take more than new fangled disinfectants to ward off the armies of ants, cockroaches, flies and praying mantis that invade our home every day but anything is worth a go. White ants are the biggest pest — the whole place is running alive with them. I shouldn't be surprised to wake up one morning

*and find a six foot ant hill in the middle of the 'sit-
ting' room, hardly the right name for it — the dogs
could use it for the same thing dogs use lampposts
in England. Give me the gentle insects of home any
day — this Africa is definitely meant for those with
the pioneering spirit instilled in them and I think
I'm getting it, too, for I wouldn't change a moment
of it . . .*

CHAPTER 22

Jack of All Trades, Master of None

Of my many jobs the easiest is the issuing of licences for hunting, fishing and driving. One should also have a licence for living in Wankie — no, actually, one should receive a medal for living in Wankie.

1st August 1955

. . . The police give the driving test, if the candidate passes, and they usually do, they come to me. I congratulate them, get them to fill in the forms, and then I make out their licence. They can then drive wherever they like legally. I say legally because we have many cases where the driver doesn't bother to get a licence, causes an accident, receives a hefty fine and is banned from driving for a year. Mind you my test took about five minutes in the pouring rain — not exactly a stiff examination.

On one memorable day the Chief Inspector's wife, the same lady who Calamas accused of stealing groceries, took the driving test for the second time.

"I can drive! I don't have to beg for lifts any more. What a relief!" The Chief Inspector's wife was positively glowing.

Anderson dropped a note in my lap: *Can you imagine what would happen to the young constable if she failed again?*

The constable who had given the test, his assignment completed, left by the back door to collect his motorbike.

I handed her the form and with a shaking hand she began to fill it in. And then the unimaginable happened. She'd forgotten to put the brake on in her car. It was careening down the kopje, gathering speed as it went.

Ndozwi rushed in, "Medem, Medem, the car — it is running away."

I rang the police.

Monty answered.

"Tell the Police Chief his car is on its way down the kopje with no one driving it and his wife has failed her test."

"Crikey — hold on." He was back in no time. "No one hurt; the car's hanging over the kopje, stopped by a tree. I wouldn't want to be in her shoes when the Inspector gets back."

The Police Chief's wife cried uncontrollably. She did not get her licence that day.

Anderson gave her a ride home.

Sherlock summed it up for all of us. "That woman's a danger to society. My advice, if anyone asks for it, is to keep her off the road and out of the grocer."

Of course, it became the subject of conversation at the Mine Club for days.

A few weeks later, in a borrowed vehicle, she took the test a third time, putting the hand brake plus the foot brake every time she was told to stop. The constable, who'd accompanied the Police Chief's wife, asked to be taken off the driving test schedule.

Her car remained in the tree until one night someone managed to get it down. It's probably in the Native compound close to the one the elephant sat on.

✉

4th August 1955

. . . I've just come back from a half round of golf and I am exasperated and exhausted. I never thought I could get into such a state over a little white ball — today it landed up in the oddest places and I spent three quarters of my game trying to find the blinking thing and then working my way out of the bundu while getting stuck behind mountainous ant hills and hidden tree roots. Half way through the game a native herd boy drove his emaciated cows across the fairway and that completely distracted my concentration not that there was much left of that anyway. Then an elephant came into view and I was petrified. If you think they look big in photographs you should see them in real life, they are enormous and this one was a bull elephant probably looking for his wife . . . the woman I was playing with told me to stand still, not move and wait for him to pass. A game is supposed to be enjoyed — this one does not fit that description. I'm giving it up.

A probation officer from Salisbury decided to pay us a visit. Why, I could not fathom. He's from the Mashonaland district, and we're Matabeleland. Still, I was curious.

"Who's on probation here?" I inquired.

"Half of Wankie," he replied.

"Don't be ridiculous."

"All right, may be not half, but quite a number. We keep track of them — we know they look for work at the mines, no one asks questions there. I'd like to have a look at your records to see if I recognize any names. When I find repeat offenders, I report them to the police. "

"What type of offense?"

"Bashing wives, bashing drunks, bashing each other," He answered.

"We've had plenty of them."

"May I have a look at your court records?"

"Be my guest." I showed him the record books on a shelf behind my desk. I kept the current one open so it never had to be moved — it weighed a ton. "If you find any names you recognize, I suggest you go to the colliery offices or the club. Good luck. Sorry I can't be of more assistance, Anderson's somewhere around, he's been here longer than me. If you have any questions, ask him."

I left and ran to the courtroom where Sherlock, not in a good mood, let me know he hadn't got all day to wait for me to turn up to take down the evidence on the case before him — theft on Rhodesian Railways.

"Where have you been?" he bellowed.

"With a probation officer."

"Has he gone?"

"Yes, sir."

"You're not in the army — forget the 'sir.' "

"Right, Your Honor."

"Stop it. Stop it now. Where's the accused?"

"Beside me," Monty indicated.

"Read the indictment."

"Fred Higgins, you are accused of grand theft on the Rhodesian Railways. What do you plead? Guilty or not guilty?"

"Not guilty."

Sherlock: "You were caught red handed with sacks full of mail, and you have the audacity to tell me you are not guilty?"

"I was helping the post office."

"Rubbish. The post office has sufficient employees to collect their own sacks."

"I was informed they were short-handed."

"What you take me for, a blithering idiot?"

Higgins looked as if he were itching to answer that question, but obviously thought better of it. He held his tongue.

I looked around the courtroom while Sherlock shuffled papers. Extra benches had been brought in to accommodate the motley mob who'd come to hear the proceedings — all white, of course — all cohorts of Fred Higgins and probably just as guilty.

Sherlock: "You like reading other people's letters?"

"Not really."

"But you do enjoy cashing other people's checks?"

No answer.

"Enough. You are remanded in custody. Take him away."

Monty reminded Sherlock there was only one cell at the police station for European prisoners, and he'd put a drunk in there for an overnight stay.

"Then shove this one in with him and stop wasting my time."

The dog whined.

The Magistrate stood.

The messenger bellowed, "God save the Queen!" and Court was over for the day.

✉

15th August 1955

. . . I have just left court with a notebook full of short-hand to be transcribed. The accused looked just like a Teddy Boy shipped over here from Clapham Junction and his followers the same. They have been stealing sacks of letters removing anything that might enclose a cheque. The case will go to Bulawayo because we are limited in the sentences we can hand out. Sherlock is foaming at the mouth — he'd like to have the lot of them rounded up and sent back from whence they came but that's not going to happen. Must stop this letter — He's just stormed in.

Sherlock: "Have you ever . . . I feel like a lion with no teeth. I'd give him ten years if I had the authority. I had to hold myself back from wiping the smirk off Higgin's face. If you ask me, they're all in on the game. Make sure the police get him on the train to Bulawayo tomorrow. I don't want him hanging around here, bragging."

CHAPTER 23

Give it a Miss

At times it seems there are more wild animals walking about in Wankie than there were in the game reserve. We had an armadillo the size of a small bus ensconced in the courtroom, waiting for the Land Development Officer to return it to the wild. An ostrich frightened the life out of shoppers at the Calamas Everything Store. Baboons were raiding every dustbin they could find. Monkeys got into our huts. Elephants wanted to play golf with us. Bats flew at night.

I'd been chased round the Mine Club swimming pool by a hunting spider, bitten by mosquitoes, had a bout with malaria and made friends with chameleons and lizards. I deplored the snakes and stayed away from the crocodiles. Overall I'd settled down in Wankie "as if to the manor born." Relatives in Johannesburg wrote letters and sent articles to prove their concern. This one was published in the *Rand Daily Mail*:

> *. . . if you are contemplating a trip to the Victoria Falls by all means go by train and for the same price you can take a few days in Bulawayo and while there visit the Matopos where Cecil Rhodes is buried. Catch the train again and go up to the Falls — it will stop at a few small stations on the way. If you wish to go the Wankie Game Reserve*

you should make reservations at one of the lodges there. The small town of Wankie has nothing to offer the tourist other than a colliery and unless coal interests you, give it a miss.

If that didn't say it all, nothing would.

Still, I was becoming quite attached to the place. True, it had little going for it, but what little it had was extraordinary, especially for me at the Native Commissioners Office. We were all outsiders in Africa trying to assimilate, wanting to make a difference and experiencing a way of life we would not otherwise have known. I'm pleased we didn't listen to the relatives who said I would never adapt. I'm glad we didn't give it a miss.

16th August 1955

. . . crime has died down considerably and the office is reasonably quiet. I try every day to reason with our black brethren but I fear it is a task well beyond me. I start off each morning with all good intentions but before very long my patience gets thrown to the winds. For example a young African came today with a note from a doctor to say he had cancer of the foot and refused to allow the doctor to operate. For one solid hour I pleaded with him but all he could say was 'if they cut off my toes how will I be able to walk?' So he'll go back to his kraal where the witch doctor will sacrifice a few of the Africans oxen which he can ill afford to lose and in less than six months he'll be as dead as the oxen the witch doctor has feasted upon. You see the European's task especially where I work in the Native Commissioners Office can be heartbreaking. They come for help, you offer a chance of saving

their life and what happens — they refuse European Medicine. We are not the ogres we are made out to be. I can vouch for that. We do what we can . . . On a different note, though not necessarily brighter, our dogs have chewed up my Jewish Cookery book — the chances of getting another one here are non-existent — we'll have to wait til we get back to South Africa to get an authentic bowl of chicken soup unless you can send one out to me. Did I tell you that every recipe in Rhodesian cook books begin with: 'First Wash Your Hands.'

I am now in charge of all things medical. Why, I'm not sure. There are medical facilities here. I have lepers to transport, malnourished children to place with missionaries, scurvy sufferers and pregnant women referred to the Native hospital, barren women wanting to become pregnant. The latter have tried everything from devouring placentas to pleading with the spirits. If they were married and could not conceive, the lobola had to be returned.

I'd witnessed irate husbands wanting to rid themselves of barren women, elders saying their kraal had been cheated, mothers pleading for their daughters and fathers saying under no circumstances would they return what's been traded — they'd probably eaten most of it anyway. If they are married under Native law, they bring a piece of paper — which few of them could read — stating they had entered into an agreement. If not, all hell breaks loose and the counting begins. Five goats, only three offered — not as many oxen or cows, forget the chickens, they're long gone. Fights break out, men needing to prove they're virile, females wanting to rid themselves of the men, parents ashamed, Chiefs requiring settlements, Sherlock demanding peace and quiet, and me stuck in the middle of it all. Eventually, Ndozwi moves them outside. How come they always blame the female for infertility?

Sometimes the situation gets out of hand, knives are drawn, blood spilled, and we have to call the police, who in their own sweet time wander up the kopje to sort things out. The next Native Court day I hear the bloke who's drawn a knife explain he's been cheated and all he wants is a wife who can provide a child, preferably male. And that's where Sherlock comes in.

"Justice? Do you think knifing the father of your betrothed deserves leniency? If I live to be a hundred, I will never understand what you people want." Sherlock was on his soap box, again. "Violence is not the answer to having or not having a baby. I would venture to say it might be exactly the opposite." He glanced at the interpreter who wasn't taking much notice. "Wake up, man!"

The interpreter got the message.

"The accused will spend one week in the Wankie jail. He will then be released to his kraal, where he will try once more to impregnate his woman. If there is no indication of a child growing in her womb after four or five months, he may return to this office and we will grant a severing of their vows."

Try interpreting that.

The accused showed no sign of interest in the woman he was supposed to impregnate.

The hospital had set up Native TB clinics in the rural areas between Bulawayo and Wankie, and for some reason it was my job to get the TB patients to the clinics while at the same time keeping my distance. I left it to the messengers to take down their names and where they came from, while I made arrangements. As for the lepers, I knew I couldn't catch what they had, I just needed to make sure I called the Wankie railway station to order the special compartment to take them to the leper colony in Ngomahuru — I couldn't afford to make that mistake again.

✉

5th September 1955

. . . Sherlock has gone out on river patrol rounding up all the natives evading tax — half of them have no idea what tax is or why they're supposed to pay and they shouldn't have to — that's my humble opinion. He isn't coming back 'til Thursday giving me time to catch up on my work. I have just finished typing out a case of a European fellow who fathered a child with a native girl and thereby producing a coloured baby. Such a travesty is considered worse than murder in this country and the fellow will probably be ostracized for life if he stays around here. The mother has been awarded ten pounds in damages and five shillings a month maintenance. For sure he'll disappear, the mother can whistle for the five bob promised. We'll never be able to find him neither will she . . . The nuns from the Catholic mission have arrived, five of them in their long black habits. How they can stand to wear those wimples, those clod hopper shoes, actually their entire penguin outfits in this heat I didn't know. In the Matabeleland district I knew of two Catholic mission stations. There were others too — Methodist, Baptist, Wesleyan, and probably more. Only the Catholics wore the habit.

"I am Sister Mary Ellen. We have come to ask if you can remove the lions that come every night and frighten us and the Natives we feed every day."

"You need to speak to one of the rangers in the game park, they should be able to help," I responded.

"The rangers tell us they are only in charge of the lions in the game park. We haven't come all this way to be sloughed off by you." Arms folded, Sister Mary Ellen stood her ground. "Have you ever been close to a lion? They smell like the devil, and they eat our chickens."

I've always had a problem with missionaries, and it's not because I'm not of their religion. It's what they do and the way they do it. The Baptists baptise, the Catholics proselytize, and the Methodists find a river to dunk bodies in. The latter in Africa can be very dangerous: bilharzia, crocodiles and countless other perils. No matter what, they gather nonbelievers into the fold and count how many converts they've made. They send the statistics back to England or Scotland, or wherever they came from, and praise God for his help in converting the heathen. And that's my point: the converted Natives are given Coca-Cola and a bun once a week. The rest of the week they return to their kraals to worship the spirits of their forefathers, just as they had done for centuries before the arrival of the white man. The missionaries are committed humanitarians, but they should not take away the gods of the indigenous people and replace them with their God.

While the nuns stood there, I called in the Land Development Officer, who informed me lions were not his job.

Anderson agreed. They weren't his job, either.

Sherlock arrived from his river expedition covered in mud, telling me he'd seen enough wildlife to last him a lifetime and he couldn't care less about a lost old lion visiting a mission station. After he'd downed a double whisky and mellowed a bit, he said he'd send a hunter friend to the mission to shoot the bloody thing.

"'Tis against God's teachings to kill," Sister Mary Ellen declared. "If that's your only solution, we'll deal with it ourselves."

"Then keep it as a pet and see how far that gets you," Sherlock called out as he disappeared into his office.

The nuns piled into their lorry and disappeared down the kopje.

Weeks later a note came by messenger from the mission station.

I took it in to Sherlock.
"Open the damn thing," he ordered.

The good Lord took charge of our problem, which is more than I can say for you or Her Majesty's Government.

Chapter 24

Witchcraft in Lupane

✉

21st September 1955

. . . two rapes coming up this week which means I have to type up the cases — blushing to my roots and making out it doesn't worry me in the least now. The other crimes are petty, burglary, wife beating (European), witchcraft (African spell hasn't worked wants money back). Sitting outside my office is a bloody great big Alsatian — police trained. I have been given instructions not to go anywhere near it which means I'm stuck here until someone moves it, uh uh — it's come in to say hello — help. It's teeth are enough to frighten the living daylights out of me but for the sake of my pride I'll sit here and whisper good doggy, good doggy until I'm blinking well hoarse. "Someone please remove this creature, it won't stop licking me."

Her Majesty's government had to address the situation promptly or a baby would surely be sacrificed. A chief and his headman came to the Native Commissioners to request an ndaba at their kraal close to Lupane, a small town on the road to Bulawayo. A near-white baby with African features had been born to a Native woman. Those who lived in neighboring kraals said the child was a bad omen and should be done away with.

Sherlock informed them if anything happened to that child they would be indicted for murder.

The Chief promised he would watch over both the child and its mother, but he couldn't vouch for how long.

Sherlock agreed to attend the ndaba and insisted I go with him. We left the following day.

It was about an hour's drive from Wankie to Lupane — Sherlock in the driving seat of the Land Rover, me beside him and Ndozwi at the back. After stopping a few times to ask the way to this particular kraal, we finally found it off the strip road and down a dirt track.

The Chief and his headman were waiting for us. We were given sawn off tree trunks to sit on. The mother and her baby were brought to us.

Sherlock asked to hold the baby. It was indeed white, but not the white of a European child. A boy, it had yellowish kinky hair, pinkish colored eyes and couldn't have been more than a month old.

The mother looked terrified.

Ndozwi interpreted: "They have not seen child like this before. He is causing trouble. They are frightened. The headman of nearest kraal came to see child. They said child is bad thing it must not be allowed to live."

Sherlock gave the child back to its mother.

She placed it at her breast, where it suckled contentedly.

"The child is an albino." Sherlock knew it meant nothing to them.

"The red you see in his eyes is not because he is a bad spirit or sent from the devil — that's nonsense — it's a symptom of his condition. You will not kill him. You will not cast spells upon him, and you will keep him safe."

"They do not want him in their kraal. They want him sent away."

"What about his mother?" I asked.

"She must go too."

I looked at Sherlock, hoping he'd have an answer. He wasn't forthcoming.

"How about a mission?" I suggested, "Surely we could find one to take them."

Sherlock perked up. "Brilliant. Bring me the father of this child."

"She does not know the father. She has three husbands. One is the Chief."

"You see, that's the problem," Sherlock pointed out to me. "She probably does know but won't say. And if it is the Chief, it's obvious why they want to get rid of the child. I don't like the feeling here."

Sherlock spoke directly to the Chief. "Do you believe this to be your child?"

This time Ndozwi adamantly interpreted: "No, No, No. It cannot be his child."

It was obvious this was not a matter of pride, it was one of control. The Chief would be thrown out with the mother if he owned up, and anyway there was no way of telling who had fathered the poor thing. He had many children, none of them white.

He spluttered on for a good five minutes.

Ndozwi didn't have to interpret; it was obvious the Chief would never accept the child as his. Then the Chief and headmen spoke among themselves. Next they called for their witch doctor. He arrived — more discussion. When they came to a conclusion, they followed the witch doctor's commands. They made a circle and placed the woman and the baby in the middle together with the witch doctor. He took the baby, lifting it high above his shoulders and began to chant.

"How long am I supposed to sit here and wait?" It was getting hot, and Sherlock had heard enough.

"He is separating the bad spirit from the kraal," Ndozwi told us.

"We're taking them with us with or without their permission."

"Witch doctor must finish, then we go," Ndozwi advised.

I held the baby while his mother went back to her hut to collect the few belongings she had. She came back, retrieved her child and, without looking at the Chief or the headman, followed us to the Land Rover. She appeared lost and ashamed. My heart went out to her.

I asked Sherlock what he planned to do.

"What you suggested. They'll be sent to one of the missions. Catholic might be the best. They look upon this sort of thing as a gift from God. Good thinking, young lady. Good thinking."

We drove the rest of the way in silence, except for the intermittent sobs from the mother clutching her baby. Ndozwi kept his distance from her. Obviously, he too felt the spirits had played a nasty trick.

26th September 1955

. . . while I am typing this letter there is a native at my desk strenuously denying a charge of forgery — I have the check in front of me, the one he is supposed to have forged — he must think we're all fools — I could have done a better job — he will be taking a little trip down to the police and will no doubt appear in my criminal record book next week. I must say I feel sorry for these fellows — they have so little and we have so much — I wonder if we will ever see equality here — where it won't be necessary for a native to forge for money. I hope so . . . Now I have to sort out a native husband and wife. She says she married him he says he didn't marry her, he married someone with the same name. That's a new one on me. I suppose it will land up with the two cows and countless goats being given back to

the father of the girl and a native divorce costing
one pound and they'll have a fight over who pays.
I just wish they'd sort these matters out in their
kraals without bringing their animals up here . . .

A note arrived from the Animal Husbandry Officer stating that
a rabid dog has been found and I was to issue a tie up order.
How do I word this one?"

"Write what you like as long as it makes sense," Sherlock
advised.

"How about this?"

Tie up order. *All dogs must be kept on leash.*

"Not strong enough — you must add "or be shot on sight.""

"That's a bit harsh."

"Never mind, make a few copies and get the messengers
to distribute them. On the other hand, if the dog belongs to
someone, and is not on a leash, they will be fined."

"How much?"

"Five pounds. Have you ever seen what rabies looks like —
probably not. Well, it's awful in animals and deadly in humans.
If diagnosed early it can be dealt with a very unpleasant injection in the stomach."

So, now I have his dog tied to my desk on one side, Anderson's dog tied on the other side and that 'orrible Alsatian tied
up outside. A number of children have been bitten and are
receiving those very unpleasant injections.

Permits to move dogs out of Wankie have been curtailed,
which has resulted in umpteen disgruntled owners coming to
me every day asking what they are supposed to do with their
animals when they have to go out of town, even suggesting we
set up an arrangement for them here.

"This is not a kennel," Sherlock reminded me. "Tell them to
stay home or have their dogs put down. We can't have a rabies
breakout here. It's bad enough we have to deal with all the other
contagious diseases." He reminded me that, since I'm already in

charge of all permits and licences, dealing with dogs and their owners shouldn't be much of a chore.

"But you can't expect them to shoot their own pets?" I complained.

"Let me be more explicit. Rabies infects the brain and the spine and is almost always fatal unless treated before symptoms appear. The symptoms are dreadful, foaming at the mouth, going crazy, unable to stand up . . . Would you like me to continue?"

"I've heard enough. I got the message."

"Then stop feeling sorry for the dogs and start being concerned for the humans."

8th October 1955

I have just had to pay myself a fine because one of our dogs was seen untied in the front of our rondavels — luckily the cook got hold of it before someone shot it. Isn't that ironic? I, in charge of issuing permits had neither a permit nor a tied up animal, it just didn't cross my mind that the order was meant for me too. Haven't said anything to anyone here, they don't need to know . . . It looked as if it was going to rain yesterday but the rains did not come. The rainy season should begin soon, there is hardly anything green for miles around and the ground is parched and the dust flies everywhere and being on a coal seam you can imagine the colour everything is. Oh — just heard the tie up order has been made valid for three more months — more rabid dogs have been found — what a place this is, what with rabies, black water fever, malaria and umpteen other fever causing germs lurking everywhere I wouldn't believe the travel agents when they promote healthy holidays in the Wankie Game Reserve.

This coming week will be a nightmare because of the

criminal cases scheduled. There are six natives in the local jail all awaiting preliminary examinations for alleged crimes — murder, arson, housebreaking, theft, culpable homicide and rape. The police are complaining. Sherlock's complaining and I'm complaining because we're all overworked and underpaid. But then there are times when we have nothing to do other than sit and watch the fans go round . . . why can't criminals stagger their crimes?

CHAPTER 25

Lightning Strikes

The rainy season has finally begun again. The rain is falling, not in drops but in sheets, and I've yet to find an umbrella strong enough to bear the weight of its continuing deluge. The rivers have overflowed their banks and we are cut off from both Bulawayo and the Falls until the rain subsides. Everything is damp: damp paper, damp people and damp dogs, although the latter are now inside looking out and happy to be inside while the tie up order is still in place.

Insects of every kind have come out of hiding. Mosquitoes feast on anyone they could find — frogs squashed on the kopje road, live ones jump in and out of puddles, and ticks are abundant on livestock. Added to all this, they tell me when it lets up a bit the flying ants arrive — a delicacy for the Natives and a nuisance for us.

Locust stew

"You should try them, full of protein, got a sort of nutty flavor, just don't think of them as ants," Anderson suggested.

"Thank you, no. They are all yours."

One afternoon, in a really bad storm, I answered the telephone, which happened to be near my window. A streak of lightning hit the phone and threw me across the room. I landed on Anderson's desk and watched as the phone disintegrated on the floor in front of me.

A clap of thunder loud enough to awaken the dead followed.

Natives waiting outside huddled together.

Sherlock rushed out of his office. "Telephone's out again . . . " then he saw me bent over Anderson's desk and realized what happened. "What's with you?" He gave me a hand up and checked to see if I was all right.

"A bit shaken. Otherwise, I think okay."

"Come, we'll have a cup of tea and wait the storm out, or would you like something a little stronger?"

"Tea will be fine," I replied, still a bit zonked.

"It's my fault, I forgot to tell you never to answer or speak on a phone in a storm. You're lucky it hit the phone and not you."

Sitting in his office he told me horrific electric storm stories: about the hunter who raised his gun to shoot a kudu when lightning struck him — he died, the kudu lived. Another when he was called to a kraal where lightning had struck a thatched roof, which caught fire and quickly spread, wiping out every thatched hut there.

"They blamed their witch doctor. He'd got them to perform a rain dance, the rains came and so did the lightning. It's either a drought or a deluge here. Stay off the phone. Actually, you won't have much choice — the lines will be down for days. Go home, you've had a hell of a shock."

I decided to stay. The police dockets were piling up on my desk.

✉

9th November 1955

The rabies tie up is getting to be big business. Any dog found unleashed is shot on sight and so it is not unusual to find carcasses on the wayside. The natives get beatings and the Europeans get fined consequently I am forever collecting money and the messengers are forever walloping their fellow brethren, (let me add that nothing gives them greater pleasure — inflicting pain is one of their favourite pastimes so it seems.) I hate it when I have to record the punishment of say ten or twenty lashings — it's barbaric . . . the more I live in Africa the more I realise it is meant for the African and not for the European . . . we don't understand them and they certainly haven't a clue about us.

Sherlock stood at my desk. "You have managed once again to put the Wankie Stationmaster in a panic. He has five lepers waiting on the platform. They've been there for three days. Last week one of them got on the train without any identification and got thrown off in Dett. He walked back along the railway lines to Wankie to be with his fellow lepers. I hope you realize you may be made responsible for spreading the disease."

I'd done it again, forgotten to put in an order for the leper coach. There wasn't much I could say other to apologize profusely and promise not to let it happen again. I thought it better not to tell him I was suffering from overload — in charge of everything from issuing permits to elephant hunting (a fee of one hundred pounds sterling and only one elephant per hunter), to witch doctor squabbles — and no one but me in the office.

And now, with the rains upon us: mosquitoes buzzing, villages flooded, knives sharpened, murders abundant, miners injured, rape flourishing, bilharzia rampant, crocs feeding, trains delayed, food depleted, cattle dying, goats vanishing, mealies rotting, women barren (incidentally, never a complaint about impotent men), children drowning, spirits rebellious, rivers rising, anger mounting. I had neglected the lepers or, what was worse, put other travelers at risk.

The days when there was little to do were few and far between.

✉

26th November 1955

We've had umpteen natives in here this morning suffering from T.B. How the hell we manage to stay clear of that dreaded disease is quite beyond my understanding. We are breathing in and exhaling the same air, but as I haven't got it now I don't suppose I'll get it ever, at least I hope not. Again I've managed to turn the whole of the Rhodesian Railways in to an uproar by placing yet another Leper on a train without ordering a special coach. It didn't dawn on me for one moment that the silly so and so would get in to a train full of people without saying anything. . . . next weekend we are all going to Livingstone to hear Julius Katchen — the well-known pianist. I suppose we will wine and dine at the Falls Hotel before attending the concert. Imagine going over fifty miles for an evening's entertainment. It's not so bad going there as coming back. Let's hope the road will be free of elephants and other animals that roam the bush at night.

CHAPTER 26

Car Turns Over, Dress Size Increases

On an earlier journey back from Bulawayo, shortly after we arrived in Wankie, I turned the car over. I own up now because I did not confess to the Native Commissioner or the police that I was the driver. Not that it would have been out of the ordinary — cars and trucks turn over all the time here, especially in the rainy season. I'd gone to Bulawayo with a friend who wanted to buy a dress for the upcoming Mine Managers big event. The dress I intended to wear no longer fit me, so I had a good excuse for going with her.

We'd bought lovely outfits, had a light lunch and started to make our way back. We were miles from anywhere on a strip road with no sighting of a human from the moment we'd left Bulawayo. A half hour into the drive she said her eyes were closing and would I take over.

I didn't hesitate. We changed seats and off we went. Cruising at a relatively low speed I saw something large in between the strips. I swerved to avoid it, and that's when the car — as if in slow motion — turned over and left us sitting upside down, unhurt and not quite understanding what had happened. I could not open my door, and neither would the passenger door budge.

Animals came to have a look. A giraffe towered over us. Zebras took a sniff. Warthogs ignored us completely. What I thought had been a boulder turned out to be a very large armadillo, which strolled off into the bush, not realizing his life had been saved by my jamming on the brakes.

Finally, a Native found us and came over to the car. He tried to open my door. No luck. He then went 'round to the other door and that too was stuck. He motioned he'd come back, and he returned with ten or more Natives. One of them held a long piece of metal shaped like a golf club. I'd seen one like it before — it's what they use to cut through high veldt and open windows to steal cars. He pried open my door and got me out.

I knew a few words of Ndbele and asked where the nearest concession store was.

He pointed both ways — obviously we were between two stores.

I'd forgotten my friend was still stuck in the car. I signaled to them to get her out.

Again the piece of iron did the trick.

Shaken, luckily uninjured, she emerged.

We stood there looking completely helpless.

The Natives had a discussion amongst themselves and gathered around the upside-down car. With almighty strength, five pushed on one side of the car while the other five took the weight of the vehicle as it balanced between them. Finally, they managed to get it in an upright position. It was a bit bashed on the roof and the windscreen had popped out. We were open to the elements, but, otherwise, not too bad — and, miracle of miracles, it started.

"Ngiyabonga, ngiyabonga," I told them, which meant, "Thank you, thank you." I gave them all the money I had in my wallet, and we continued on our way. One hundred and sixty miles at twenty miles an hour with me apologizing profusely and my friend on the lookout for elephants.

We arrived back in Wankie looking like two red Indians, the dust of the road covering us and the car, both inside and out.

"What took you so long?" My husband inquired.

Not a "How are you?" or a "What happened?" or an "Are you all right?" No, just "What took you so long?" Typical.

I was beginning to realize what it was going to be like being a doctor's wife from now on. Doctors can do no wrong in the eyes of their patients. Wives have to grin and bear any sharp pain or discomfort without any show of concern from the man they married.

I told him part of the story. He wasn't going to get it all, for I would never live it down, and he'd say "Women drivers," in a derogatory tone and go off on a tangent. I could have reminded him of the time he nearly ran into a warthog on the Falls Road but thought it best to shut up and have a bath instead.

5th September 1955

The next party at the Mine Managers house began in his garden and ended in his home. Not unexpected in this uninviting place where it doesn't rain for months and then while everyone is dressed to the nines having a good time, a deluge of rain comes out of nowhere and soaks us all. The new dress I bought on that fateful car turnover day dripped for the rest of the evening and probably shrunk to the size of the one I replaced it for. It was a late night so when we drove up to the Falls the next day for the Julius Katchen concert I slept most of the way. I am pleased to say most of his program was rousing for had he settled down to play dreamy, slumber music I feel sure I'd have dozed off again . . . we arrived back in Wankie after two in the morning. Much to our horror we couldn't open the door to our bedroom — the wood had swollen from the rain. I had visions of spending the night on the dirt floor. Finally one of the servants heard us shouting and came to our rescue by breaking the gauze on the hut window. Now we had the company of a selection of flying insects. Perhaps the dirt floor would have been better . . . oh, just another piece of news, you will soon be referred to as Grandma and Grandpa

*to be, I am having a baby — August 2nd expected date
... now I know why I've been feeling sick in the morning so it won't matter about the new dress shrinking
— it won't fit me in a couple of months anyway.*

Our days in Wankie were drawing to a close. David's contract
had two months to go, and neither of us cared to renew it.
I insisted our unborn child be born in England, and David
wanted to leave general medicine and head toward a degree
in cardiology. I too had a contract to fulfill, and I hoped I'd be
able to get through the remaining time without throwing up at
inconvenient moments.

Sherlock, when told of my condition gave me a hug, said jolly
good, and shoved papers in my hand. "Just got a call from a mine
supervisor — says one of his men has to marry immediately."

"What's the hurry?"

"The bride to be is nine months pregnant and she wishes to
legalize the child's birth, which appears imminent."

"Is this a Native marriage or a European one?"

"White on white," Sherlock answered, "and they are coming
up the hill as we speak. Gather the troops. We need a witness,
and they asked for a priest. Find one."

"How about a nun? We've got plenty of them?"

"Just get something that looks like a devout Christian up
here as soon as possible."

The marriage took place under the jacaranda tree outside my
office. Sister Mary Ellen dragged her bicycle up the hill and attended, complete with prayer book. Anderson found another old
bottle of champagne in a cupboard. I witnessed the ceremony,
and Sherlock, in his capacity of Magistrate, married them.

Most of the Europeans came to us for shotgun weddings,
and Sherlock never failed to repeat his favorite observation.
He told the bride, dressed in all her finery, that she looked outstanding. And outstanding she was: her belly protruding and
her legs tightly crossed as she sat in great discomfort, while I
made sure the papers were signed correctly.

She refused champagne — her new husband obviously didn't want to be there — and I had a preview of what I would look like in a few months.

Sherlock and Anderson took a swig and handed the bottle to me. I declined — if I couldn't keep down a cup of tea, I surely wouldn't manage a glass of champagne in the early afternoon. The very look at the bottle made me more nauseous.

"I'm glad you weren't in the family way before your nuptials," Sister Mary Ellen remarked, giving me one of her memorable stern looks. "In the eyes of the Lord, sexual relations before marriage are a mortal sin."

"They asked for God's blessing, it's why we asked you to join us. You are, after all, a stand-in for the Lord."

"I wouldn't put it that way," she replied but seemed chuffed with the compliment. "I'm here just to do the good Lord's work."

"And you have done it," I complimented her. I didn't let on I was in the family way. She might want to baptize the child in utero!

When you believe everything written in the Bible, as this nun had been programmed to do, then much of how we in Wankie live our lives might be considered sinful. Christians in Wankie rarely attended church. I did not observe the Sabbath. Sherlock was an agnostic and a really bad one in the eyes of the church for suggesting birth control for the indigenous population. Females of child bearing age seemed to have a baby every year, rarely with the same father.

Sister Mary Ellen told him she would say a hundred Hail Mary's on his behalf to cleanse him for his wayward mutterings.

Sherlock was not about to put up with another religious diatribe. Instead, he took Sister Mary Ellen by the hand, loaded her bike on to the back of his Land Rover and drove her in great haste back to the hospital.

Two hours later he returned, three sheets to the wind, having imbibed at the Mine Club. "Well," he slurred as he entered my office, "someone had to commemorate the occasion."

The bride gave birth that evening with Sister Mary Ellen assisting. The groom took one look at his newborn and disappeared.

"I wonder how many more kids he'll father?" I asked of no one in particular.

"None of our business," Anderson replied. "It's bad enough the Natives breed like rabbits in our district — at least they spread their seed amongst their own. A male child they acknowledge. A girl, well they'd like to shove her back in the womb to cook a bit longer."

✉

12th December 1955

I am told by my beloved husband that my sickness is psychological, that I shouldn't make a fuss, that I'm not the only girl in the world to have a baby but it is all right for him to grin like a Cheshire Cat as if he's the only man ever to father a child . . . In answer to the article in the Daily Express about whites saving money in the colonies as usual it only touches the surface. The Europeans I know, here in the Federation of Rhodesia and Nyasaland are trying to work out how anyone can save five hundred pounds per year here, because they can't. True enough salaries are high but then the cost of living is tremendous. Rents, servants, food, etc., all take a chunk of our wages. An average person here earns a hundred pounds a month (not the African of course he gets about ten pounds, food and accommodation and in our case more for his family and children). Out of our one hundred pounds come school fees, holidays (a big item if one wants to go down to the sea the nearest point being over a thousand miles) drinking, Rhodesia's main past time, smoking and partying. One has to make one's own entertainment, little is provided. True enough the Federation has a wealth of minerals but how many people want to go out into the bundu to peg their

*claims and start digging — lucrative it might be,
still a hard and lonely life for a family. An artisan,
a bricklayer can earn with overtime up to one hundred and twenty pounds a month, an office worker
an average of eighty. They don't want the collar
and tie worker here, they want the rough working
class who don't care where they live or in what
conditions they find themselves. The working class
who come out here think they've landed in paradise,
they've never had it so good, they don't care about
the thousand and one troubles and petty hatreds
surrounding them, that's not their problem, they're
here to get whatever they can out of this country. I
don't expect that the Daily Express correspondent
has mentioned anything about the tensions in Africa
because it won't be very long before the African sees
how the immigrant who comes with nothing and
lives like a lord says to himself, I want that, too.
In twenty years from now the management of the
Wankie Colliery Company thinks this whole place
will be run by the African with just a few Europeans
to guide them on their way. What then will all the
immigrants do? Wankie is only one example — there
are many more. If the bottom drops out of copper
then the whole of the Federation is sunk. It depends
on the wealth that lays to the north of us, in Kitwe,
Ndola and Mufalira in Northern Rhodesia, and if
the federation breaks up we will lose the benefit.
So my dears, my advice to you is not to pack your
bags and come to the richest empty space probably
in the world, it looks fine in the newspaper, written
by reporters who spend a few days here and then
return to civilization with only a cursory look at
what is really happening here. It isn't half as rosy
as it is painted.*

CHAPTER 27

I Survived in Wankie

The cases continue to come in, but in a few weeks time I will not be the one trying to make sense of them. Sherlock is looking for a new Clerk of the Court — someone like me, he says, someone who doesn't take him too seriously, someone who can accept his occasional tantrums.

A Native Commissioner's job can be frustrating, difficult, unappreciated and occasionally heartbreaking. An even temper is not a prerequisite. I have learned more in this hotter-than-hell, off-the-beaten-track, hardly functioning, animal-friendly, people-hostile, strangely named hole in the ground than I ever would in London or any major city in southern Africa. It cannot be taught in school, not even in college. It can only be experienced.

The average European in Africa rarely steps out of his comfort zone. He lives in the cities or small towns, has servants and doesn't give a damn where they come from. Often he treats them offhandedly and can dismiss them on a whim, knowing they can easily be replaced.

This is not the case in the Native Affairs Department, where a dedicated bunch of colonial Brits do a yeoman's job in less-than-friendly places. I am indebted to them and always will be. They opened my eyes, they stood by my side and showed me a world I would not have known had it not been for them. I think there will come a day when they'll be considered obsolete, their expertise no longer required. But until then the Native Commissioners and their assistants are needed, and those I have come across are committed to the work they have been sent out to do. They care about the tribal African. They carry out their work in a fair and proper manner. The Land Development Officers teach what they know: agriculture and animal husbandry. The BSAP police keep order both in the towns and tribal areas.

The Queen's photo hangs in our offices — she is our boss and we, the managers of the lands over which she reigns. But our days are numbered; I sense we will not be here very much longer. We have made a difference, we have shown what can be done and we have opened up a land and, in many ways, made it better. We have taught, we have shown and we have helped develop a country that, before we came, was tribal, warlike and often dangerous. We have eradicated some diseases and controlled others. We have organized game parks and protected the animals. We have built roads and brought in electricity. We have provided jobs and tried to work toward a multi-racial society. We haven't got there yet, but given time, we might.

I fear for the future at the same time I have hope for it. I will leave with both sorrow and a sense of achievement. I am glad I took a walk those many months ago when that young man in a jeep offered me a job. Who would have thought a woman of twenty-one, no longer an innocent girl, could learn so much in so short a time? Had I attended university I would not have gained as much knowledge of human nature as I have in these last two years, and I will take what I have learned and try to tell others of the Africa I came to know: Tell them the Africa of the new Federation of Rhodesia and Nysasaland could be a land of promise — if we continue to treat it and its indigenous people right. And we have to ask ourselves, when the time comes for independence — and it will — whether the indigenous Native gained more from our short stay, or did we just conquer, control and take more than that we were entitled to? I could honestly say the former holds true for all of those who worked in the Native Affairs Department.

15th March 1956

Dear Mummy and Daddy,

You can now close the file of correspondence and put it away somewhere very safe so that in years to come we can look back on pleasant and exciting memories . . . keep well and in just two weeks time we will all be together again.

Last letter from Wankie

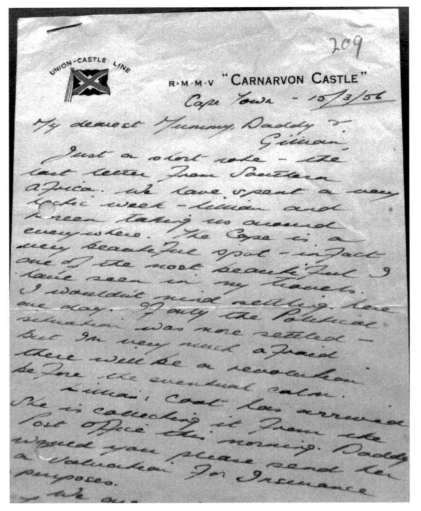

On the ship back to England

Epilogue

They say once you've spent time in Africa, it stays in your blood. It has certainly stayed in mine.

Wankie, you were my continuing education and my growing experience. You may be one of the hottest places on the African continent, perhaps the dirtiest too because of your coal deposits, but my stay there — just fifty miles from the Victoria Falls, cut off by rivers in the rainy season, bitten by malaria carrying mosquitoes, lacking shops, having an overabundance of missionaries, inhabited by alcoholics, over run by baboons, living in mud huts, far from civilization — was a wake-up call to a young woman who had lived all of her life in a London suburb.

I see it now as the opportunity of a lifetime.

It gave me insight to a culture I would only have known about in books. It gave me an understanding of primitive life that cannot be replaced by any professor or born white man living in the comforts of a city or a town. I came to Africa expecting to live in Johannesburg, a city of ease and comfort — as long as you happen to be a European, which meant white. Everyone had a least one servant.

Africans were called kaffirs or boys, the latter even if he were a man of mature years. A few whites stood up against the apartheid government or were jailed for mixing with non-whites and liberals. Many whites left the country, fighting the regime from beyond its borders.

Apart from the fact there was no job available, we could not in all good consciousness stay.

I came to Rhodesia thinking, as the doctor's wife, for a

couple of years I'd perhaps find some voluntary work to fill my time. My in-laws were right, perhaps it wasn't the place for an innocent young Londoner — not innocent of war, for I had lived through that — unaware of Africa in its truest sense. Wankie might not be everyone's cup of tea: situated where it was, the heat, the lack of decent housing, the melting road, the flying night bats, the ever-present baboons, the heavy drinkers, and the Europeans who came for the right reasons and many who came for the wrong, the lads in the Native Commissioners Office and the nuns from the convent. For me, it was my home for two precious, never-to-be-repeated years.

Looking back, I would not change a moment of it, even if we'd been offered a comfortable, three-bedroom residence in a well-to-do community, where doctors are supposed to settle with their wives. Instead, we spent time in a backward mining town in the middle of central Africa and loved every minute of it.

Thirty years later I returned to Wankie — renamed Hwange, Zimbabwe. I travelled by car on a proper road to a thriving town with shops and suburbs. It was not the same place I had left. Our two huts were still there, though not residential. Instead of mud, they were now brick. A note was attached to the same door they eventually installed for us:

AIDS Clinic — Open Every Day

Except it wasn't open that day.

The Guest House and the government quarters across the way had been replaced by bungalows. Africans could live anywhere they chose and mingled with Europeans. The Native Commissioners Office had long closed, the BSAP station was no more. The Baobab Hotel had a smart new look and the guests were sober. The kopje didn't seem so steep, and the roads weren't melting. The Hwange Game Reserve catered to visitors from all over the world, and the animals stayed within its designated area. Calamas store was still there, but far from where other shops thrived. The mine dumps were fenced off, the new hospital of my time had settled into being a bit grubby, but still functional, and nothing was separated. Independence had brought equality and a westernization of a mining town that had once been my little piece of Africa.

The letters you have read are in my possession. My mother did keep them, bearing in mind that one day they might be of interest. Some I have quoted from directly, others I have used in the body of the story.

We returned to The Federation of Rhodesia and Nyasaland in 1959 and stayed until 1964, when war was on the horizon and Europeans were leaving in droves. I did not want to leave, but for the sake of my children, I too had to go.

In the train down to Johannesburg, on our way to a new life in America, I thought over the years I'd spent in Africa in Southern Rhodesia and Northern Rhodesia, now Zimbabwe and Zambia.

I came back in the late nineties to make a film, *Journey from the Jacarandas*. We could not complete it; the country was near bankruptcy — the banks closed — we were forced to leave with a half-completed film.

It is a country that has forsaken its people. It seeks diplomatic help from the West but doesn't accept the guidance offered. It accepts without gratitude the legacy of its pioneers. It allies itself with Communist countries and rigorously denies its own history.

For a while it faltered on the edge of disaster — now that disaster is upon them. Farms have been taken from Europeans who stayed and given to politicians who know nothing about farming. Once it was the breadbasket of Africa, today there is famine in the land. The infrastructure is fast disintegrating — the President lives in a palace, his people barely survive in hovels.

Yet, this is still a land of great beauty, of gentle, spiritual people with vast potential. I know why it entered my soul and became part of who I am. We together "lived" in Rhodesia, not on an equal basis, that is for sure, but surely better for everyone then. We were on our way to a multi-racial society — we needed time, they needed time. Now those left behind struggle to survive.

Rhodesia breathed — Zimbabwe chokes.

There is no way I can bring yesterday's values forward to today. I recognize the past and the inequalities then. I see the changes, and they are not for the good. The tables have turned and I ask, "Are they really for the better?"

I heard President Mugabe address his cabinet as "comrades" and speak as a capitalist. He grows fatter as the people he governs grow thinner.

More than one African asked me, "Why did you leave? Look at us now."

I answered, "We left because you no longer wanted us."

I wish it could have been different. Unfortunately, it is what it is.

Patricia Friedberg
Sarasota, Florida, 2013

ACKNOWLEDGMENTS

No memoir is written or compiled by the author alone — it is always a joint effort for it includes not only memories but historical facts that have to be checked and validated.

My thanks go to Mary Ann Amato, my stalwart literary agent and friend, who brought the manuscript of *Letters from Wankie* to Publisher Betty Wright of Rainbow Books, Inc. To Leslie Dubow for proposing the title, *Letters From Wankie*. To Michael Peters, the noted international design consultant, for designing the front cover. To Colin Weyer (www.rhodesia.me.uk) for allowing us to include, along with those in my collection, his delightful photography. We haven't met in person but I hope to someday soon. Thanks to Rafe Bencid for the one hundred trillion Zim dollar note and the Rhodesian stamp. My gratitude to Rhodesia and Zimbabwe friends scattered throughout the world, all of whom helped jog my memory, and to Jacqueline Garber in London for keeping letters sent to her by me from Rhodesia.

Had it not been for David, there would be no *Letters from Wankie*. He died in 2005 — I can only thank him posthumously.

GLOSSARY

The following words are listed for the purpose of pronunciation and understanding. Many are Zulu in origin and were adapted by the Ndebele in the Rhodesias. If you read other texts, you may find alternate spellings because Zulu an Ndebele are not written languages.

acacia — (uh-KAY-shuh) Also known as a thorntree, whistling thorn or wattle, acacia is a genus of shrubs and trees.

Afrikaans — (Ah-free-CONS) A Low Franconian, West Germanic language descended from Dutch and spoken by 10 million people, mainly in South Africa and other African countries.

Alsatian — A dog also known as a German Shepherd.

baobab tree — (BAY-oh-bab) boab, boaboa, bottle tree, the tree of life, upside-down tree, and monkey bread tree. The species reach heights of up to ninety-eight feet and trunk diameters of up to thirty-six feet. Its trunk can hold up to 30,000 gallons of water. For most of the year, the tree is leafless and looks very much like it has its roots sticking up in the air. It can provide waterproof shelter and clothing, as well as food and water for animals and humans.

Barangwanath — (Bar-an-GWAN-ath) A non-European hospital in Johannesburg, South Africa named after a famous Cornish early settler.

Batonka — (Ba-TONK-ah) — A tribe, also known as Batonga and Tonga, from the Zambezi River valley.

bilharzia — (bill-HAR-zee-ah) Also known as Katayama fever, swimmer's itch, blood fluke and schistosomiasis. A parasitic infection contracted through contact with contaminated open bodies of water, particularly in Africa, Asia and South America.

biltong — (BILL-tong) A type of jerky made from wild game in Africa.

bob — British slang for money

Boer — (bore) The Dutch and Afrikaans word for farmer, which came to denote descendants of the Dutch or Huguenot settlers of the eastern Cape frontier in Southern Africa.

Boer Wars — Two wars, between the British and two independent Boer Republics in what is now South Africa, fought from both 1880–1881 and 1899–1902 and won by the British.

boerewors — (BORE-a-vors) A traditional South African sausage.

bonnet — The hood or front of an automobile, usually over the engine.

breivleis — (BRI-flase) An Afrikaans word for barbecue.

bundu — (BUN-do) A Bantu word for the bush or the middle of nowhere.

bush — An uninhabited, undeveloped area.

Cola Tonic — A South African soft drink.

colliery — (CALL-you-ree) A coal mine and its connected buildings.

collywobbles, the — A bellyache or upset stomach associated with nervousness.

couchette — (KOO-shet) A bed in a boat or on a train that can be folded away and used as a seat.

crikey — (CRY-key) A British slang expression of surprise or an oath, crikey is a euphemism for Christ.

dicky-bird — A British rhyming slang, meaning, not a word.

dustbin — British word for trash can or garbage can.

Fortescueweg — (FOR-tess-CUE-weg) Afrikaans for Fortescue Road.

fortnight — British expression for two weeks.

gauze — British for screen.

Gwaai — (G-why) The name of a town along the River Gwaai in Rhodesia.

Gwanda — (G-wanda) The name of a town in Rhodesia.

hou links — (HOW-lenks) Afrikaans for keep left.

ikona boneelie — (i-KONA bo-NEE-lee) An African/Native pseudonym for golf.

Ingutsheni — (in-goot-SHEN-nee) A psychiatric hospital in Rhodesia.

kaffir — (KAF-fur) Derogatory slang for an African Native.

Kalowe — (kal-OW-ee) A Mhondoro woman's name.

Kitwe — (KIT-we) A town in Rhodesia.

kopje — (cop-EE) From the Dutch, literally, a little head (in South Africa) a small hill.

kraal — (crawl) Native for a village.

lobola — (low-BO-la) The Native Ndebele word for a dowry.

lolloped — A British word that means moved slowly.

lorry — A British word that refers to a truck.

Mafeking — (MAH-fuh-king) A small town in the northeast corner of Cape Province (South Africa), where a British garrison was besieged for seven months during the second Boer War.

Mashona — (ma-SHONE-ah) A Native tribe in Rhodesia.

Mashonaland — A province in Rhodesia.

Matabele — (mat-ah-BEE-lee) A Native tribe in Rhodesia.

Matabeleland — A province in Rhodesia.

Matopos, the — (ma-TOE-pos) Short for the Matopos Hills within Rhodes Matopos National Park.

mealie — corn

medem — (ME-dem) Zimbabwean pronunciation of madam.

Mdala — (m-DA-la) An old man.

Mhondoro — (mon-DOOR-oh) A respected female spiritual guardian of the tribe.

moeni spoeg nie — (MO-nee spoke nee) An Afrikaans word meaning do not spit.

Mosi-o-tunya — (MO-see-o-TONE-ya) A Native word for Victoria Falls, meaning, the smoke that thunders.

mopani — (em-PA-nee) A fly indigenous to Africa.

Mufalira — (MOO-fa-LEER-a) A town in Rhodesia.

Native Affairs Department — In 1894 the British South African Company established the Native Affairs Department to be responsible for the welfare of Native Africans living on tribal trust lands. Head of the Department was the Administrator in Council, beneath him was the Secretary for Native Affairs. Under the Secretary were the two Chief Native Commissioners of Matabeleland and Mashonaland. Under the Chief Native Commissioners were Native Commissioners who were responsible for the administration of their tribal districts and sub-districts. They were assisted by Assistant Native Commissioners with the organization having its own native police force.

ndaba — (n-DA- ba) Zulu for a meeting.

Ndola — (n-DOLE- a) A town in South Africa.

Ndowzi — (n-DOZE- wee) The Head Messenger's name.

Ngamahura — (m-GAH-ma-WHO-rah) A leper colony in Rhodesia.

ngangas — (n-GANG-gas) Healer.

ngiyabonga — (n-GYEE-a-BON-ga) Zulu for thank you.

nkos — (n-KOSS) — A superior, master, chief, sir.

nkosikas — (n-KOSS-see-kas) — Madam, queen, wife.

Nyaminyami — (N-yah-min-YAH-mee) Spirit of the Zambezi River.

Nyasaland — (Ny-ASSA-land) Once a province of Rhodesia, now known as Malawi.

Panyesani — (PAN-ya-SA-nee) A person's name.

pillion — British for the passenger seat behind the driver on a motorcycle.

pudding — British word for dessert.

rondavel — (ron-DA-vel) A thatched circular hut or other building, usually with a conical thatched roof.

Sangomas — traditional African healers; witch doctors.

scarpers — getting away quickly.

Shonas — (SHOW-nas) A Rhodesian tribe.

sudza — (SUD-za) A porridge made of cornmeal.

sweets coupons — During and following World War II in Great Britain, sweets were rationed because of a sugar shortage due to restriction on imports . Coupons were issued; sugar rationing allowed for two ounces of sweets for the E coupon and four ounces for the D coupon.

Teddy Boy — A 1950's British expression attributed to a tough youth subculture, mainly from unskilled backgrounds, who wore a modified style of turn-of-the-20th-century clothing.

three penny bit — (THRUP-enny bit) A British coin worth three pennies.

torch — The British word for flashlight.

tote — The British word for total.

tyre — The British spelling of a tire on any vehicle.

unyoko umama — (un-YOKO u-MAMA) Your mother.

vanette — The British word for a small van.

veldtschooners — The Afrikaans word for bush boots.

Wange — (WANG-ee) Chief of the Hwange area.

Wankie — (WANK-ee) A coal mining town in Southern Rhodesia, now renamed Hwange, Zimbabwe. The Wankie Coal Field, one of the largest in the world, was discovered there in 1895. The town is named after the chieftain of Zwange, who is now called Chief Hwange. The town was known as Wankie until 1982.

Welensky, Sir Roy — Second Prime Minister of The Federation of Rhodesia and Nyasaland, from 1956–1963.

yarmulke — (YA-mul-ka) A skullcap worn by religious Jews.

About the Author

Author Patricia Friedberg was born in London, attended The Henrietta Barnett School and The London School of Journalism. Married to a South African doctor, they resided first in a mining town in Southern Rhodesia, Wankie (Hwange), and then later in both Northern and Southern, known now as Zambia and Zimbabwe, settling finally in Salisbury, Southern Rhodesia, now known as Harare.

Her government connections as Clerk of the Court for the Native Commissioner's Office in Wankie allowed her to travel freely into the rural/bush, accompanied by a photographer. Her articles were published in Rhodesian News and produced as Tribal Documentaries by the then newly formed RTV (Rhodesian Television). In the 1960's, with political unrest intensifying in Rhodesia and for the safety of their children, the Friedbergs reluctantly left Africa to settle in the United States, first in Baltimore, Maryland and then in Milwaukee, Wisconsin.

Patricia attended a play writing course at Marquette University, where her first work, *Masquerade*, a play about Apartheid, won the Play Writer's Award. She was later commissioned to write two docu-dramas — *Dwellings*, about living in different places, and *Babble*, about gossip in small towns — both for Wisconsin Public Television, MPTV. She established a Children's Theatre Arts Program in Milwaukee and produced and directed two works of her own: *Is Today Tomorrow?*, a child's confusion about why tomorrow never comes, and *Hamba Wena*, an African piece about a child finding his way in a foreign land. Two further plays were performed at Marquette: *Tenement*

Torment, about the effect of living in overcrowded conditions, and *Through the Eye of the Little Green Buddha*, a large green sculpture on stage the presence of which has an increasing effect on those who find it either menacing or comforting.

Patricia wrote for the *Milwaukee Jewish Chronicle* and moderated *People of the Book* for WTMJ-TV (NBC affiliate), for which she interviewed major celebrities, politicians and well-know personalities in the art and music world.

Studying script writing independently, she wrote the screen-play "Journey from the Jacarandas," a feature film that began filming in Zimbabwe in 1997–98 and was interrupted due to civil unrest and government sanctions.

Children's books, titled *Dear Sammie* and *Dear Jake: A letter from a grandparent to a child of divorcing parents*, were co-authored with her daughter Adrienne Meloni and published in 2008.

21 Aldgate, published in July of 2010, tells of British class divide in the 1930s and a young woman's journey from a working class background to the upper class environment in the wealthy confines of London's Chelsea. Set during the buildup and into the Second World War, *21 Aldgate* depicts the effect war has on a family living in the East End of London and on the main characters. The author has given over a hundred book talks in both the UK, the USA and on the *Queen Mary 2*. *21 Aldgate* continues to enjoy great success as a book club favorite and is praised by its readers and critics.

Patricia Friedberg can be reached through her websites and agent's email: PatriciaFriedberg.com, www.21aldgate.com, legaciesliterary@gmail.com and Facebook.